MW00973660

BAPTISTWAY ADULT BIBLE STUDY GUIDE

LARGE PRINT EDITION

The Gospel of Luke

GOOD NEWS OF GREAT JOY

PERRY LASSITER
LEIGH ANN POWERS
MIKE SMITH
RANDEL EVERETT
RONNIE AND RENATE HOOD

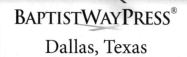

BAPTISTWAYPRESS®
Dallas, Texas

The Gospel of Luke: Good News of Great Joy—BaptistWay Adult Bible Study Guide®
Copyright © 2009 by BAPTISTWAY PRESS®.
All rights reserved.
Printed in the United States of America.

No part of this book may be used or reproduced in any manner whatsoever without
written permission except in the case of brief quotations. For information, contact
BAPTISTWAY PRESS, Baptist General Convention of Texas, 333 North Washington,
Dallas, TX 75246–1798.

BAPTISTWAY PRESS® is registered in U.S. Patent and Trademark Office.

Scripture marked NIV is taken from The Holy Bible, New International Version (North
American Edition), copyright © 1973, 1978, 1984 by the International Bible Society.
Used by permission of Zondervan Publishing House. Unless otherwise indicated, all
Scripture quotations in unit 1, lessons 1–4, are from the New International Version.

Scripture marked NASB is taken from the 1995 update of the New American
Standard Bible®, Copyright © The Lockman Foundation 1960, 1962, 1963,
1968, 1971, 1972, 1973, 1975, 1977, 1995. Used by permission. Unless otherwise
indicated, all Scripture quotations in unit 2, lessons 5–7; unit 4, lessons 13–16;
and unit 5, lessons 17–18, are from the New American Standard Bible.

Scripture marked NRSV is taken from the New Revised Standard Version Bible,
copyright 1989, Division of Christian Education of the National Council of
the Churches of Christ in the United States of America. Used by permission.
All rights reserved. Unless otherwise indicated, all Scripture quotations on
the back cover and in "Introducing the Gospel of Luke: Good News of Great
Joy" and unit 3, lessons 8–12, are from the New Revised Standard Version.

BAPTISTWAY PRESS® Management Team
Executive Director, Baptist General Convention of Texas: Randel Everett
Director, Education/Discipleship Center: Chris Liebrum
Director, Bible Study/Discipleship: Phil Miller
Publisher, BAPTISTWAY PRESS®: Ross West

Cover and Interior Design and Production: Desktop Miracles, Inc.
Printing: Data Reproductions Corporation

First edition: December 2009
ISBN-13: 978-1-934731-40-6

How to Make the Best Use of This Issue

Whether you're the teacher or a student—

1. Start early in the week before your class meets.

2. Overview the study. Review the table of contents and read the study introduction. Try to see how each lesson relates to the overall study.

3. Use your Bible to read and consider prayerfully the Scripture passages for the lesson. (You'll see that each writer has chosen a favorite translation for the lessons in this issue. You're free to use the Bible translation you prefer and compare it with the translation chosen for that unit, of course.)

4. After reading all the Scripture passages in your Bible, then read the writer's comments. The comments are intended to be an aid to your study of the Bible.

5. Read the small articles—"sidebars"—in each lesson. They are intended to provide additional, enrichment information and inspiration and to encourage thought and application.

6. Try to answer for yourself the questions included in each lesson. They're intended to encourage further

thought and application, and they can also be used in the class session itself.

If you're the teacher—

A. Do all of the things just mentioned, of course. As you begin the study with your class, be sure to find a way to help your class know the date on which each lesson will be studied. You might do this in one or more of the following ways:

- In the first session of the study, briefly overview the study by identifying with your class the date on which each lesson will be studied. Lead your class to write the date in the table of contents on page 9 and on the first page of each lesson.

- Make and post a chart that indicates the date on which each lesson will be studied.

- If all of your class has e-mail, send them an e-mail with the dates the lessons will be studied.

- Provide a bookmark with the lesson dates. You may want to include information about your church and then use the bookmark as an outreach tool, too. A model for a bookmark can be downloaded from www.baptistwaypress.org on the Resources for Adults page.

- Develop a sticker with the lesson dates, and place it on the table of contents or on the back cover.

B. Get a copy of the *Teaching Guide,* a companion piece to this *Study Guide.* The *Teaching Guide* contains additional Bible comments plus two teaching plans. The teaching plans in the *Teaching Guide* are intended to provide practical, easy-to-use teaching suggestions that will work in your class.

C. After you've studied the Bible passage, the lesson comments, and other material, use the teaching suggestions in the *Teaching Guide* to help you develop your plan for leading your class in studying each lesson.

D. You may want to get the additional adult Bible study comments—*Adult Online Bible Commentary*—by Dr. Jim Denison (president, The Center for Informed Faith, and theologian-in-residence, Baptist General Convention of Texas) that are available at www.baptistwaypress.org and can be downloaded free. An additional teaching plan plus teaching resource items are also available at www.baptistwaypress.org.

E. You also may want to get the enrichment teaching help that is provided on the internet by the *Baptist Standard* at www.baptiststandard.com. (Other class participants may find this information helpful, too.) Call 214–630–4571 to begin your subscription to the printed or electronic edition of the *Baptist Standard.*

F. Enjoy leading your class in discovering the meaning of the Scripture passages and in applying these passages to their lives.

Writers of This Study Guide

Perry Lassiter wrote unit one, lessons one through four. A graduate of Baylor University and of Southern Baptist Theological Seminary, he is a veteran curriculum writer. He served as a pastor for more than forty-five years and continues to preach and to serve churches as an interim pastor. He is a member of First Baptist Church, Ruston, Louisiana. For many years he taught a pastor's class in Sunday School and continues to teach a men's Bible class.

Leigh Ann Powers, the writer of unit two, lessons five through seven, is a member of First Baptist Church, Winters, Texas, where her husband serves as pastor. She is a graduate of Baylor University (B.S.Ed) and of Southwestern Baptist Theological Seminary (M.Div.) She and her husband, Heath, have two children.

Mike Smith wrote unit three, lessons eight through twelve. Dr. Smith serves as pastor of First Baptist Church, Murfreesboro, Tennessee. He is a graduate of Belmont University and of Southern Baptist Theological Seminary (M.Div., Ph.D.). He serves as a trustee of Belmont University and enjoys writing, editing, and golf.

Randel Everett is executive director, Baptist General Convention of Texas. Dr. Everett wrote unit four, lessons thirteen through sixteen. He formerly served churches in Texas, Arkansas, and Virginia and also served as founding president of the John Leland Center for Theological Studies, Arlington, Virginia. He earned master's and doctoral degrees from Southwestern Baptist Theological Seminary.

Ronnie and Renate Hood wrote unit five, lessons seventeen and eighteen. Dr. Ronnie W. Hood II was serving as senior pastor of Fellowship Baptist Church, Longview, Texas, when he wrote these lessons. He is a graduate of Samford University, Birmingham, Alabama. Dr. Renate Viveen Hood is associate professor of Christian Studies at the University of Mary Hardin-Baylor, Belton, Texas. She earned medical science degrees in the Netherlands. The Hoods studied at New Orleans Baptist Theological Seminary, where Ronnie earned M.Div., Th.M., and Ph.D. (Church History) degrees, and Renate earned M.Div. and Ph.D. (Biblical Studies and Greek) degrees.

The Gospel of Luke: Good News of Great Joy

DATE OF STUDY

UNIT ONE

Jesus' Birth and Childhood

UNIT TWO

Preparing for Ministry

UNIT THREE

Jesus' Ministry in Galilee

Introducing

THE GOSPEL OF LUKE:
Good News of Great Joy

Joy from Beginning to End

From beginning to end, joy is prominent in the Gospel of Luke. The angel said to Zechariah concerning Zechariah's promised son, "You will have joy and gladness, and many will rejoice at his birth" (Luke 1:14).[1] Elizabeth, pregnant with John, said to Mary, "For as soon as I heard the sound of your greeting, the child in my womb leaped for joy" (1:44). Mary, pregnant with Jesus, sang, ". . . My spirit rejoices in God my Savior" (1:47). The angel told the shepherds, "Do not be afraid; for see—I am bringing you good news of great joy for all the people" (2:10).

Jesus instructed his disciples about facing persecution, "Rejoice in that day and leap for joy, for surely your reward is great in heaven" (6:23). Later, "the seventy returned with joy" after their successful mission (10:17). Jesus told of the joy of a woman finding a lost coin (15:6), of the joy of the angels and of God when a person returns to God (15:7, 10), and of the joyous celebration led by a father whose long-lost son returned (15:24).

The Gospel of Luke further tells of the joy of disciples realizing Jesus had been resurrected (24:41). Indeed, in the final scene of Luke's Gospel, the disciples "worshiped him, and returned to Jerusalem with great joy" (24:52).

The Gospel of Luke has other special emphases that radiate from this theme of joy. In Luke's Gospel we can hear, in effect, this invitation from Jesus: *Come to the party God is having—all of you. Yes, I really mean you.* So Luke's Gospel shows Jesus reaching out to all people, which means to all kinds of people. In Luke, Jesus demonstrated special concern for people who were considered second-class in one way or another. Included in this definition were people who didn't keep the Jewish traditions, people whom the religious leaders considered sinners. Included as well were people who were in fact sinners. Other people considered second-class were the poor, women, and people who were otherwise oppressed. Jesus affirmed and reached out in love and acceptance to them all. Everybody wasn't joyful about this, but Jesus shows us that God was—and is.

Why the Longer-than-Usual Study

This study of the Gospel of Luke is longer than our usual studies. Why? Our present curriculum plan is to provide a study of one of the Gospels each year, with the first use beginning in December (although a church or class can choose to conduct the study at any time, of course, since it is undated). This plan enables us to provide an emphasis on the beginning of the gospel story at Christmas time. In addition, many churches and classes like to have the Scripture study on Easter to be on Jesus' resurrection. Therefore, for this study of the Gospel of Luke, the opportunity presented itself to lengthen the study of this long book just a bit in order to have the study extend from the Christmas season to the Sunday of Easter and thus be helpful to churches and classes who use this study during that time frame.

So, because of the time of the first release of this study, we have given focused attention to the portion of the Christian year between the Sundays leading up to Christmas and the Sunday of Easter. Having eighteen sessions will enable many churches and classes to follow Jesus from the rejoicing at his birth to the rejoicing at his resurrection, climaxing the study with the celebration of Easter.

Developing the Study

In developing this study further, the foremost concern has been to let the Gospel of Luke speak for itself rather than to impose ideas on it. (This concern applies to all our BaptistWay Bible studies, whatever the portion of the Bible being studied.) Within that concern are such factors as these: passages that move the story along on the journey from Jesus' promised birth to his resurrection while following the contours of the Gospel of Luke itself; events and teachings that appear only in Luke; and passages that apply most directly to life today. Further, the units of study are organized to reflect the organization of the Gospel of Luke.

So, unit one of our study consists of four lessons on Scriptures dealing with Jesus' birth and childhood (1:1—2:52). Unit two consists of three lessons on "Preparing for Ministry" (3:1—4:13). Unit three provides five lessons on passages on "Jesus' Ministry in Galilee" (4:14—9:50). Unit four provides four lessons on a large section in Luke's Gospel that is unique to this Gospel, "Journeying to Jerusalem" (9:51—19:27). The study concludes with a unit of two lessons on "Jesus' Death and Resurrection" (22:14—24:53).

UNIT THREE: JESUS' MINISTRY IN GALILEE

Lesson 8	Fulfilled Today?	Luke 4:14–21
Lesson 9	Jesus' Radical Message	Luke 4:22–30
Lesson 10	Called to Gather People for the Kingdom	Luke 5:1–11
Lesson 11	Jesus' Life-Altering Instructions	Luke 6:17–46
Lesson 12	Where Forgiveness Leads	Luke 7:36–50

UNIT FOUR: JOURNEYING TO JERUSALEM

Lesson 13	A Narrow Door, a Limited Time	Luke 13:22–35
Lesson 14	Priority Matters	Luke 14:1–24
Lesson 15	Coming to the Party?	Luke 15:1–2, 8–32
Lesson 16	A Fatal Mistake	Luke 16:19–31

UNIT FIVE: JESUS' DEATH AND RESURRECTION

Lesson 17	Crucified—for Us	Luke 23:1–26, 32–49
Lesson 18	Resurrected—for Us	Luke 24:1–10, 33–39, 44–48

Additional Resources for Studying the Gospel of Luke[2]

Craig L. Blomberg. *Jesus and the Gospels*. Nashville, Tennessee: Broadman & Holman Academic, 1997.

Darrell L. Bock. *Luke*. Volume 1. Baker Exegetical Commentary on the New Testament. Grand Rapids, Michigan: Baker Books, 1994.

Darrell L. Bock. *The NIV Application Commentary: Luke*. Grand Rapids, Michigan: Zondervan Publishing House, 1996.

Fred B. Craddock. *Luke*. Interpretation: A Bible Commentary for Teaching and Preaching. Louisville, Kentucky: John Knox Press, 1990.

R. Alan Culpepper, "The Gospel of Luke." *The New Interpreter's Bible*. Volume 9. Nashville: Abingdon Press, 1995.

Craig A. Evans. *Luke*. New International Biblical Commentary. Peabody, Massachusetts: Hendrickson, 1990.

Craig S. Keener. *IVP Bible Background Commentary: New Testament*. Downers Grove, Illinois: InterVarsity Press, 1993.

Richard Rhor. *The Good News According to Luke*. New York: The Crossroad Publishing Group, 1997.

A.T. Robertson. *Word Pictures in the New Testament*. Volume II, The Gospel of Luke Nashville, Tennessee: Broadman Press, 1930.

Robert H. Stein. *Luke*. The New American Commentary. Volume 24. Nashville, Tennessee: Broadman Press, 1992.

Ray Summers. *Commentary on Luke*. Waco, Texas: Word Books, 1972.

Charles H. Talbert. *Reading Luke: A Literary and Theological Commentary*. Revised edition. Macon, Georgia: Smyth & Helwys Publishing, Inc., 2002.

Malcolm Tolbert. "Luke." *The Broadman Bible Commentary*. Volume 9. Nashville: Broadman Press, 1970.

NOTES

1. Unless otherwise indicated, all Scripture quotations in "Introducing the Gospel of Luke: Good News of Great Joy" are from the New Revised Standard Version.

2. Listing a book does not imply full agreement by the writers of these lessons or BAPTISTWAY PRESS® with all of its comments.

UNIT ONE

Jesus' Birth and Childhood

This study begins with events we generally associate with the Christmas season, with all its bustle and activities. You may be engaging in this study during this season. No matter when you are studying these passages, though, don't let the flurry of activities in your life stifle your Bible study. Rather take time to dig into these lessons and discover new things about Jesus' birth and childhood.

The Gospel of Luke begins with Luke's telling us that he had made careful inquiry to discover the truths of Jesus' life and was now passing them on. According to Acts, Luke was a long-time companion of Paul.

Luke then described two annunciations. The angel Gabriel appeared and spoke to the father of John the Baptist and to Mary the mother of Jesus, announcing the births of the two. John was called to be the forerunner, announcing the coming of Jesus the Messiah.

Then Luke told the familiar story of Jesus' birth, including the angelic revelation and visit from the shepherds. Next Luke gave us a significant story from Jesus' childhood.

Get ready, for in this unit the Gospel of Luke will show us how God broke into and spoke to the devout Hebrew world of the first century.[1] Listen for how God continues to speak to our world, too.

UNIT ONE: JESUS' BIRTH AND CHILDHOOD

Lesson 1	Ending the Long Wait	Luke 1:1–25
Lesson 2	Bringing Fullness of Hope	Luke 1:26–56
Lesson 3	Proclaiming the Savior's Birth	Luke 2:1–20
Lesson 4	Committed to God's Purpose	Luke 2:39–52

NOTES

1. Unless otherwise indicated, all Scripture translations in unit 1, lessons 1–4, are from the New International Version.

LESSON ONE
Ending the Long Wait

MAIN IDEA

God's promise of a child to Zechariah and Elizabeth began to end the long wait for the fulfillment of God's promise of Messiah.

QUESTION TO EXPLORE

What are you waiting for?

STUDY AIM

To describe the significance for your life of the angel's promise to Zechariah and Elizabeth

QUICK READ

The angel Gabriel appeared to the elderly priest Zechariah to announce that he and his wife would conceive and bear a son, although both were past their child-bearing years. With this announcement, the Lord was preparing John the Baptist to announce the coming of the Messiah.

As the pastor of a couple who desperately wanted to have a child, I listened to their frustrations that they could not conceive. I shared with them that our second son had some birth problems, and the doctor advised us not to bear another child. So we approached the Baptist children's home and were approved for adoption. I told the couple that we felt our adoptive daughter was just as much our child as our other two children. The couple explored their options and eventually adopted a son of their own. Many times after that, they thanked me and told of the joy their child brought them.

Although that couple was not as old as Zechariah and Elizabeth, the arrival of a long-hoped-for son brought great satisfaction. Perhaps you or someone in your life has had a similar experience of fulfilled hope. Yet God fulfilled their desires in order to reach a broader world—a world of sin that he was about to impact.

LUKE 1:1–25

[1] Many have undertaken to draw up an account of the things that have been fulfilled among us, [2] just as they were handed down to us by those who from the first were eyewitnesses and servants of the word. [3] Therefore, since I myself have carefully investigated everything from the beginning, it seemed good also to me to write an orderly account for you, most excellent Theophilus, [4] so that

you may know the certainty of the things you have been taught.

⁵ In the time of Herod king of Judea there was a priest named Zechariah, who belonged to the priestly division of Abijah; his wife Elizabeth was also a descendant of Aaron. ⁶ Both of them were upright in the sight of God, observing all the Lord's commandments and regulations blamelessly. ⁷ But they had no children, because Elizabeth was barren; and they were both well along in years.

⁸ Once when Zechariah's division was on duty and he was serving as priest before God, ⁹ he was chosen by lot, according to the custom of the priesthood, to go into the temple of the Lord and burn incense. ¹⁰ And when the time for the burning of incense came, all the assembled worshipers were praying outside.

¹¹ Then an angel of the Lord appeared to him, standing at the right side of the altar of incense. ¹² When Zechariah saw him, he was startled and was gripped with fear. ¹³ But the angel said to him: "Do not be afraid, Zechariah; your prayer has been heard. Your wife Elizabeth will bear you a son, and you are to give him the name John. ¹⁴ He will be a joy and delight to you, and many will rejoice because of his birth, ¹⁵ for he will be great in the sight of the Lord. He is never to take wine or other fermented drink, and he will be filled with the Holy Spirit even from birth. ¹⁶ Many of the people of Israel will he bring back to the Lord their God. ¹⁷ And he will go on before the Lord, in the spirit and power of Elijah, to turn the hearts of the fathers to their children

and the disobedient to the wisdom of the righteous—to make ready a people prepared for the Lord."

18 Zechariah asked the angel, "How can I be sure of this? I am an old man and my wife is well along in years."

19 The angel answered, "I am Gabriel. I stand in the presence of God, and I have been sent to speak to you and to tell you this good news. 20 And now you will be silent and not able to speak until the day this happens, because you did not believe my words, which will come true at their proper time."

21 Meanwhile, the people were waiting for Zechariah and wondering why he stayed so long in the temple. 22 When he came out, he could not speak to them. They realized he had seen a vision in the temple, for he kept making signs to them but remained unable to speak.

23 When his time of service was completed, he returned home. 24 After this his wife Elizabeth became pregnant and for five months remained in seclusion. 25 "The Lord has done this for me," she said. "In these days he has shown his favor and taken away my disgrace among the people."

Luke Introduces the Story (1:1–4)

The story begins in the secular world of Herod the Great. Unlike most other religions, biblical faith takes place in history, in particular times and specific places. In this case, the Gospel of Luke takes us to Israel where Herod the Great was king. As did the historians of that day, Luke assured his readers he had been careful to research his material and present an accurate account.

Luke 1:1 begins, "Many have undertaken. . . ." We don't know to whom Luke was referring here. Was Luke referring to the Gospel of Mark and perhaps also to the Gospel of Matthew? Many Bible scholars believe Luke had access to the Gospel of Mark, which he (and Matthew) used as a framework or outline. Many also consider Matthew to have been written earlier than Luke.

Tradition says that Luke was a Greek physician who traveled with Paul. In Colossians 4:14, Paul refers to him as "the doctor" or "physician" (KJV). The Bible is silent about Luke's background, but at one point in Acts, the writer began to use the word *we* as though he had joined Paul's group (Acts 16:10). If so, he would have had a number of opportunities to hear first-hand accounts from both Paul and other disciples. Since many years had passed since Jesus' earthly ministry, Luke perhaps wanted to put the information down so it would not be lost as the first generation died out.

Luke addressed both his Gospel and the Book of Acts (the second volume of the same history) to a man named Theophilus, which means *friend of God*. Many have speculated about the identity of this recipient. Some feel he was a wealthy or important man who perhaps backed Luke financially in his writing. Some feel he was a Greek or Roman official, although Jews also bore that name. The fact is, we can only speculate and be grateful that Luke produced the Gospel for him.

Luke may also have expected Theophilus to pass on the book to a local church. Or, perhaps Luke made a copy to share with his own congregation. At any rate, at some point a church read Luke's story and began to pass it around to other churches. We might imagine small groups of believers gathered in house-churches as someone read aloud these inspired words. Perhaps visitors with writing skills copied the Gospel for their home churches.

The Book of Luke is a *gospel*, an account of the good news of what God has done in Jesus Christ. From the very beginning Luke sought to communicate that message. He began by saying this account was trustworthy, and Theophilus could trust what he set down therein. In fact, part of Luke's purpose was for the reader to have confidence in his faith, based on knowledge of the life and teachings of Jesus. Perhaps this search for truth is the first great desire Luke addressed.

Unfilled Desires (1:5–7)

For 400 years since Malachi, no prophet had spoken. The Jews speculated on the coming of a promised Messiah. Many expectations centered on a military or political leader who would deliver them from the Roman occupation. But God seemed quiet. Then, an elderly priest entered the temple, and the world began to change.

Zechariah and Elizabeth were past child-bearing age. They had prayed for a child, but a child had not yet been given to them. They likely had given up. Note that this couple was devout, pious, and poor. Luke's story swoops down from Herod the Great to the poor and includes not only a priest but his wife. Throughout Luke, we will see a strong emphasis on the people society often shut out: the poor, the outcast, widows, orphans, and women in general.

Zechariah was a priest, not a high priest, but still a descendant of the first priest, Aaron. Zechariah's wife shared his Aaronic background. Even their service and devoutness left them empty in a vital part of their lives, however.

Children were considered a blessing and a reward from the Lord. For a woman to be barren implied to some that she and her husband were being punished.

Angelic Vision (1:8–20)

Each morning, the priests for that day's service gathered at the temple, and a *lot* was cast. Some think the *lot* was actually two different-colored or marked stones known as *Urim and Thummim*. The high priest may have carried them in a pocket of his garment. He would reach in and select a stone. The stone selected answered a question *yes* or *no*. Although some consider the action as chance, the Jews of that day felt that God himself made the choice.

On this day, the lot chose which priest had the honor to enter the temple to make an offering at the altar. Zechariah was chosen, likely the only time in his life. Surely he was both awed and excited as he entered into what he thought of as the very presence of God.

Zechariah's task that day was to clean the ashes from the altar of incense and replace them with fresh incense. The task was not difficult and normally did not take long. What was special for the aged priest was really a daily routine, except on this day. How many times has God broken into his world in times that were expected to be routine? Perhaps you have gone to church and encountered the Lord in an unexpected and transforming way.

When Zechariah looked, he saw an angel standing by the altar. Zechariah was afraid. The angel's first words, though, were, "Do not be afraid" (Luke 1:13). Almost every appearance of angels in the Bible is marked by fear. Their first words were often, *Don't be afraid*. Much present-day talk and writing about angels is sweet and sentimental. The biblical reality could not be more different. Angels are messengers of God. They seem to appear suddenly, as if appearing from nowhere. That suddenness was in itself startling. But, an element of holiness about the angel stimulated a sense of awe. To say Zechariah was startled is too mild. He was terrified!

The angel told the priest his prayers were answered (1:13). Apparently Zechariah and his wife had implored God over many years to give them a child. No answer had come. We often feel that if the Lord does not answer immediately, or at least soon, the Lord doesn't hear our prayers. Yet the Bible reminds us repeatedly that God keeps a different schedule from ours. For what have you grown impatient?

The angel explained to Zechariah that his son would be unusually special, a servant of the Lord. He would be the fulfillment of Malachi's prophesy (Malachi 4:5–6) that said an Elijah-like leader would return to prepare the way for the Messiah. Zechariah was to name his son *John* (Luke 1:13). The boy would be a delight to his parents, and many in the nation would rejoice because of him (1:14). God's Holy Spirit would fill him from birth, and he would become a great spiritual leader in God's eyes. His preaching would turn the hearts of many to the Lord in preparation for the coming of the Messiah.

Zechariah had trouble believing the angel. He asked how he could believe the angel's message since he and his wife were well past child-bearing age. I can imagine the angel increasing his volume as he declared emphatically, "I am Gabriel. I stand in the presence of God . . ." (1:19). Gabriel was not an average angel (whatever that may be) but came from the very throne of God with a divine message. To drive his point home, the angel declared that Zechariah would be unable to speak until the child was born.

Meanwhile, the crowd of worshipers outside the building was growing concerned. Zechariah's job was simple. So he should have been in and out much sooner. When he did come out, he was signaling with his hands but could not speak. The crowd perceived he had seen some kind of vision.

After Zechariah's team of priests completed their service time, he returned home. Before long, Elizabeth became pregnant. The discovery brought her great joy, but we wonder whether she understood the place in history her son would have. Her praise centered on what God had done for her and the effect it would have on the opinion others held of her. She had felt disgraced in public opinion because she had been childless.

Yet, a new era had begun. A child was born. Soon Gabriel spoke again, and another child was on his way.

Implications and Actions

1. God often works quietly behind the scenes. A couple conceiving is a normal event. Yet each conception opens a new world of possibilities. God has a purpose for every person, whether he or she knows it or not. For some, God has critical roles for them to play in his kingdom.

2. Don't give up on God. In high school, I had a prayer list of lost people. Over many years I saw evidence that each one on the list found Christ. The list included young and old, Jews and skeptics.

3. The daily chores of temple service were chosen by lot. Yet God was behind the choice. Some feel there are no accidents but that coincidences are the fingerprints of the Holy Spirit.

4. Don't forget the joy. We should allow ourselves to enjoy what God gives us! Throw a party!

GABRIEL

In Jewish tradition, there are three archangels: Michael, Gabriel, and Raphael. The first two appear in the Bible (Gabriel, Luke 1:19; Michael, Revelation 12:7). The word *angel* means *messenger, one who is sent*. Angels usually bear crucial messages from God. Many of the messages have an impact on both the recipient and the world. In the first two chapters of Luke's Gospel, Gabriel brought birth announcements to both Elizabeth and Mary.

APPLICATION

- Make a personal prayer list. Include people you know and are concerned about. Pray for each person daily, and thank God as your prayers are answered.

- Reflect on your life. At what points can you discover the hand of God working? Share that news with someone this week.

- What are you waiting for? Are you also praying and working to that end?

QUESTIONS

1. In reading from a Bible study I had written recently, my wife asked me the question I had proposed for the reader, "What are the next major life-altering decisions facing you?"[1] She made me think deeply as a result of my own question. So against that background, I want to ask a similar question: What major event are you waiting for?

2. Now take it a step further. Are you waiting for God or someone else to act? If so, are you neglecting to take actions now to help bring it to pass?

3. How impatient are you for God to answer your prayers? Are you stalling in your life until God acts?

4. How quickly are you disappointed when God doesn't answer immediately? Do you continue in faithfulness?

NOTES ————————————————————————

1. *The Gospel of Matthew: Hope in the Resurrected Christ* (Dallas, Texas: BaptistWay Press, 2008), lesson 4, question 1, p. 53.

LESSON TWO

Bringing Fullness of Hope

MAIN IDEA

God brings fullness of hope in the Child promised miraculously to Mary and to God's people.

QUESTION TO EXPLORE

What seemingly impossible act does God want to make happen in your life today?

STUDY AIM

To identify blessings God wants to bring into life through the Child promised in a seemingly impossible manner to Mary

QUICK READ

The angel Gabriel appeared to the virgin Mary and announced that she would miraculously conceive and give birth to the Messiah God had promised.

Have you experienced the excitement of expecting a baby? We had been married six months and discovered a baby was coming as Christmas approached. I went out and bought the smallest pair of baby shoes I could find and hung them on the tree. Surprisingly (to me), when our son arrived, the shoes were way too big. But, the next year, I put a small football under the tree for my four-month-old boy! Remember the excitement surrounding any new birth as you read and study this Scripture.

LUKE 1:26–56

26 In the sixth month, God sent the angel Gabriel to Nazareth, a town in Galilee, 27 to a virgin pledged to be married to a man named Joseph, a descendant of David. The virgin's name was Mary. 28 The angel went to her and said, "Greetings, you who are highly favored! The Lord is with you."

29 Mary was greatly troubled at his words and wondered what kind of greeting this might be. 30 But the angel said to her, "Do not be afraid, Mary, you have found favor with God. 31 You will be with child and give birth to a son, and you are to give him the name Jesus. 32 He will be great and will be called the Son of the Most High. The Lord God will give him the throne of his father David, 33 and he will reign over the house of Jacob forever; his kingdom will never end."

34 "How will this be," Mary asked the angel, "since I am a virgin?"

35 The angel answered, "The Holy Spirit will come upon you, and the power of the Most High will overshadow you. So the holy one to be born will be called the Son of God. **36** Even Elizabeth your relative is going to have a child in her old age, and she who was said to be barren is in her sixth month. **37** For nothing is impossible with God."

38 "I am the Lord's servant," Mary answered. "May it be to me as you have said." Then the angel left her.

39 At that time Mary got ready and hurried to a town in the hill country of Judea, **40** where she entered Zechariah's home and greeted Elizabeth. **41** When Elizabeth heard Mary's greeting, the baby leaped in her womb, and Elizabeth was filled with the Holy Spirit. **42** In a loud voice she exclaimed: "Blessed are you among women, and blessed is the child you will bear! **43** But why am I so favored, that the mother of my Lord should come to me? **44** As soon as the sound of your greeting reached my ears, the baby in my womb leaped for joy. **45** Blessed is she who has believed that what the Lord has said to her will be accomplished!"

46 And Mary said:

"My soul glorifies the Lord

47   and my spirit rejoices in God my Savior,

48   for he has been mindful

of the humble state of his servant.

From now on all generations will call me blessed,

49 for the Mighty One has done great things for me—

holy is his name.

50 His mercy extends to those who fear him,
from generation to generation.
51 He has performed mighty deeds with his arm;
he has scattered those who are proud in their inmost
thoughts.
52 He has brought down rulers from their thrones
but has lifted up the humble.
53 He has filled the hungry with good things
but has sent the rich away empty.
54 He has helped his servant Israel,
remembering to be merciful
55 to Abraham and his descendants forever,
even as he said to our fathers."
56 Mary stayed with Elizabeth for about three months and
then returned home.

Gabriel's Announcement to Mary (1:26–38)

We can easily imagine Mary was excited. After all, she was
engaged and would be married to Joseph within the year.
Likely, her parents had arranged the marriage with Joseph's
parents, perhaps years earlier. But she had now become for-
mally engaged, which meant the bride price had been paid
and, in many respects, she was legally bound to her fiancé.
To break the engagement would require divorce. Usually the
wedding followed in about a year. Until the week-long wedding, the couple would live separately with their parents.

In that day, couples were married and treated as adults at puberty. Boys were considered men around the age of twelve or thirteen and were apprenticed to their father or another man to learn a trade. Joseph might have been an apprentice carpenter. Mary might have been about thirteen to fifteen years old, looking forward to marriage and a family. She might have even hoped to be the one chosen to bear the Messiah as many Jewish girls of that day (and later) wished.

On a day that began normally for Mary, everything suddenly changed for her and Joseph (and, for that matter, the whole world) when Gabriel appeared. The angel first greeted her as "highly favored" and told her, "The Lord is with you" (Luke 1:28). His greeting disturbed her greatly, and so he reassured her, telling her not to fear.

Gabriel went on to explain that she was going to conceive and bear a child. She was to name the child *Jesus*. The Hebrew of the name (see small article, "The Name *Jesus*") meant *the Lord saves*. Her son's mission was to be the Son of the Most High as well as to assume the throne of his ancestor David. His kingdom would be everlasting and would never end.

Mary objected. She asked in effect, *How can I be pregnant? I've never experienced sex and will not until I'm married* (1:34). Gabriel answered, *God himself will cause the seed to be implanted in you through his Holy Spirit. The child will be holy and called the Son of God* (1:35).

Gabriel continued speaking to the girl and told her that her relative Elizabeth was also miraculously pregnant. Elizabeth was too old to bear children, and yet she was in her sixth month. The angel concluded by pointing out that nothing is impossible with God (1:37).

We can now begin to see why the Lord chose Mary. She replied that she was the servant of God, and she was willing for the angel's message to come to pass. Mary showed an incredible willingness on the part of a young teen who had no idea of all the implications her decision would have.

Mary's Visit to Elizabeth (1:39–45)

Gabriel had told Mary of Elizabeth's pregnancy. Mary must have been almost overwhelmed by this new experience, and so she sought a kindred spirit to share her feelings. Elizabeth greeted her young relative with great joy. Elizabeth told Mary that as soon as Mary greeted her, Elizabeth's baby leaped in her womb (1:44). Elizabeth called Mary *one blessed by God* (1:45) and felt honored by her visit. Indeed, she gave her a more honored place as "the mother of my Lord" (1:43).

Elizabeth apparently had gained insight from the day she first became pregnant. At that point, she thought first of the new respect people would give her. As Zechariah's story of the angel sank in, Elizabeth began to realize that their family was becoming an important part of God's covenant dealings with Israel. She also recognized Mary as playing the most important role of all the mothers in the land.

Elizabeth added a further blessing on Mary, recognizing and sharing her belief in the faithfulness of God. Elizabeth recognized that God would carry out what he had promised.

Mary's Song (1:46–56)

Mary then spoke or sang a song of praise to the Lord. She said she would magnify the Lord from the depths of her heart. She called God her "Savior," a reminder to us that the Lord is behind all of the activity we know as *Christmas*. She again pointed out that God remembered her "humble estate" (1:48). She did not feel worthy or entitled to such an honor. Rather she received it as God's undeserved, gracious gift.

Mary's thoughts then turned to the mightiness of God and to God's dealings with his people and to her in particular. She stood in awe that the Almighty had focused on a simple girl to bless her powerfully. She foresaw that future generations would recognize her blessedness.

Mary thought of the history of Israel. She remembered God's strong arm to aid his people. God had the power to make and break kings. He was (and is) active in the history of the world. She also praised God for God's kindness to the poor and those in trouble. Note again that Luke's Gospel emphasizes the need of the helpless more than any other Gospel.

Mary also connected her Lord with the God of Abraham (1:55). She set herself in the context of God's dealings with his people Israel.

Mary remained with Elizabeth for several months before she returned home. The sharing of the stories and faith of the two women may well have strengthened them both for supporting and training their two sons.

The Birth of John the Baptist (1:57–80)

The background passage continues to the end of the chapter and describes the birth of John the Baptist. The Scripture says the family and neighbors wanted to name the baby after his father, but Elizabeth insisted on the name John (1:58–60). Since *John* was not a family name, they pressed Zechariah for his opinion. He asked for paper and wrote, "His name is John" (1:63). As soon as Zechariah did this, he could speak again, and his speech was in praise of the Lord.

Implications and Actions

What do you feel youth are capable of doing or becoming? This lesson shows that God entrusted a vital portion of his plan of salvation into the hands and lives of at least one teenager. Many teens are already fine Christians. Some have discovered God's plan for their lives in vocational Christian service. Let's give them steady encouragement and challenges, knowing that the Spirit is also working in their lives.

As a rule, Baptists have failed to appreciate Mary, perhaps in reaction to Roman Catholicism's over-emphasis. Yet she deserves a place of honor among Christians as an example of faith and devotion.

The virgin birth is a basic tenet of Christian faith. For us the doctrine tends to speak of the divinity of Christ. Yet for the early church it spoke equally of the humanity of Jesus. Taken together, the two emphases remind us that Jesus Christ was fully divine and fully human.

The virgin birth was a miracle from God. This intervention of the Lord into his world reminds us that God still can and does work wonders among us.

THE NAME *JESUS*

The name "Jesus" comes from the Greek New Testament (*Iesous*) through Latin (*Iesus*) to English. It was translated from the Hebrew name *Joshua* or *Yeshua*. Almost certainly the people of Jesus' day called him something like *Yeshua* or *Yoshua*. The name appears, with variations, several times in the Old Testament. Most famous is probably Moses' lieutenant, Joshua. The name was common in Jesus' day as evidenced by numerous appearances in other writings outside the Bible. The name means *the Lord saves* and was given to Jesus by the angel Gabriel (Luke 1:26–31; see Matthew 1:21).

Applying This Lesson

To put this Scripture into practice:

- Expect God
- Look for God as you go through the day
- Pray to God regularly and often
- Attempt something great for God

QUESTIONS

1. Last week we asked, "What are you waiting for?" Now take the subject a step further. What are you expecting God to do? Are you open to God's activity in your life?

2. Mary, a teenager, sought out Elizabeth, a much older woman. How much interplay between generations is there in your family and in your church? What can you do to promote more intergenerational friendships?

3. This chapter in the Gospel of Luke has several songs or poems. How do you express your excitement about your faith and your experiences with God?

FOCAL TEXT
Luke 2:1–20

BACKGROUND
Luke 2:1–20

LESSON THREE

Proclaiming the Savior's Birth

MAIN IDEA

God's promise to Mary came to pass in the birth of the Savior, Christ the Lord.

QUESTION TO EXPLORE

What does it mean to celebrate and proclaim the birth of the Savior who is Christ the Lord?

STUDY AIM

To summarize what it means to celebrate and proclaim today the birth of the Savior who is Christ the Lord

QUICK READ

Arriving in Bethlehem for Joseph to be enrolled in a census, Mary delivered her firstborn son. In the fields, angels revealed the birth to a group of shepherds, who immediately went to Bethlehem to find the child.

When I was a child, my parents read the story of the birth of Jesus every Christmas morning. My wife and I continued that tradition while our children were still at home. Since then we have varied the tradition. Most recently, we gathered the extended family group, about twenty people, for our biggest Christmas gathering and sang two or three carols. Do you have similar traditions you observe at Christmas time? If not, why not start some?

LUKE 2:1–20

¹ In those days Caesar Augustus issued a decree that a census should be taken of the entire Roman world. ² (This was the first census that took place while Quirinius was governor of Syria.) ³ And everyone went to his own town to register.

⁴ So Joseph also went up from the town of Nazareth in Galilee to Judea, to Bethlehem the town of David, because he belonged to the house and line of David. ⁵ He went there to register with Mary, who was pledged to be married to him and was expecting a child. ⁶ While they were there, the time came for the baby to be born, ⁷ and she gave birth to her firstborn, a son. She wrapped him in cloths and placed him in a manger, because there was no room for them in the inn.

Shepherds & Angels

8 And there were shepherds living out in the fields nearby, keeping watch over their flocks at night. **9** An angel of the Lord appeared to them, and the glory of the Lord shone around them, and they were terrified. **10** But the angel said to them, "Do not be afraid. I bring you good news of great joy that will be for all the people. **11** Today in the town of David a Savior has been born to you; he is Christ the Lord. **12** This will be a sign to you: You will find a baby wrapped in cloths and lying in a manger."

13 Suddenly a great company of the heavenly host appeared with the angel, praising God and saying,

14 "Glory to God in the highest,

and on earth peace to men on whom his favor rests."

15 When the angels had left them and gone into heaven, the shepherds said to one another, "Let's go to Bethlehem and see this thing that has happened, which the Lord has told us about."

16 So they hurried off and found Mary and Joseph, and the baby, who was lying in the manger. **17** When they had seen him, they spread the word concerning what had been told them about this child, **18** and all who heard it were amazed at what the shepherds said to them. **19** But Mary treasured up all these things and pondered them in her heart. **20** The shepherds returned, glorifying and praising God for all the things they had heard and seen, which were just as they had been told.

An Enrollment (2:1–5)

God moves in surprising ways to get people where he wants them. In this case, God was moving Joseph and Mary to the city of Bethlehem so Jesus could be born there. Why? Because long ago the Lord had promised David that one of his descendants would always be available to sit on his throne (1 Kings 2:4; 8:25). The Jewish people expected God to send this promised king as a messiah to free his people, and Bethlehem was the town where David's family lived. So, having the Messiah born in Bethlehem restated God's covenant with David. Further, Micah had prophesied (Micah 5:2) that an eternal ruler would come from Bethlehem.

Caesar Augustus was the Roman emperor. He ruled over most of the known world and was considered a god by many. Herod was under Augustus and king over Judea and some surrounding areas. He died in A.D. 4. Herod had been good to the Jews, even helping rebuild the temple. Still they hated him because he was not a Jew and because he ruled for the Romans. Herod had a difficult time during his last years because of family plots against him to seize his kingdom. He became suspicious and cruel, executing many of his own family.

One report says that when Quirinius became governor of Syria, the first thing he did was take a census (Luke 2:2). This enrollment was used for many purposes, but especially as a tax roll. What was unusual about this enrollment was that people had to return to their original family homes rather than signing the documents where they were then living. As a result, Joseph and Mary had to go to Bethlehem. The couple had to travel about eighty-five miles (by the most direct route) to reach Bethlehem. Surely the trip would have been hard on Mary in light of her pregnancy.

A Birth (2:6–7)

Luke described the birth of Jesus in simple terms. He used many more words to relate the announcements to Elizabeth and Mary. He included the responses of both of the women and of Zechariah. Now, in beautiful language Luke described simply the most important birth in history.

Mary "gave birth to her firstborn son." The word "firstborn" implies Mary had more children later, and Scripture indeed refers to Jesus' brothers.[1] She wrapped the new child in cloth bands, which were common coverings for newborns. The manger was a feeding trough for animals.

Many scholars now believe they were staying in a *caravanserie*, referring to a sort of campground, perhaps surrounded by walls or hedges within which travelers stayed and tended to their animals—horses, mules, and camels. The place likely was crowded because of the census, and Mary and Joseph could find only a corner of this area in which Mary could give birth. The inn was already full.

You've probably heard many sermons and comments about there being no room in the inn. The speaker often goes on to query whether we are making room for the Savior in our lives. But a point we must not overlook is that Jesus was born anyway. When we try to shut God out of our lives and leave only a crack for God to get in, God's humility and love let God take what space we give him. Where do you find God striving to get into your life? Are you trying to shut God out?

Shepherds and Angels (2:8–20)

Shepherds were low on the social scale in Palestine. But in keeping with Luke's effort at every opportunity to show that the Savior was for everyone, Luke carefully depicted the role of the shepherds in the nativity experience. Shepherds were not allowed in the temple to worship without first undergoing a rigorous ritual cleansing. Yet God sent his angels directly to the shepherds at work. No one is so low or sinful as to lie outside God's love and care.

These men apparently were camping out in the fields to take care of their flocks. Suddenly the night sky broke open, and an angel appeared to the men. This angel is not identified by name, but only as "an angel of the Lord"

(Luke 2:9). Such a title appears a number of times in the Old Testament.[2]

The glory of the Lord is not described, but we may imagine it as a sense of brilliance and brightness with an aura of holiness. In the Old Testament, the glory of the Lord is often associated with the tabernacle or the temple. The Lord had transformed the pasture into a place of worship.

As usual with angelic appearances, the shepherds who experienced it were terrified. Again as usual, the angel's first words were, "Do not be afraid" (2:10). Artists have painted the scene as a lovely and inspiring one. Perhaps we await the painter who can somehow include the sense of awe and even terror.

The angel continued to say he was bringing *good news*. These words are the foundation of our word *gospel*. In a sense, the heavenly visitor said, *I am preaching the gospel to you.*

What was the good news? A Savior had been born nearby in the city of David, Bethlehem, probably visible on a nearby hilltop. Note the words "to you" (2:11). The angel was empha-sizing the birth of the Child was for them. The wealthy and the powerful often assume good news is for them. The Gospel of Luke emphasizes that the child was born for all. See the small articles "Savior," "Christ," and "The Lord" for explanations of the three titles given the Child.

A heavenly choir singing praise to God joined the angel. Their song included a blessing for those on earth. The King

James translation is "good will toward men" (2:14), but *to people of good will* is likely a better translation. As Jesus did in the Beatitudes (Matthew 5:1–12; Luke 6:20–22), the song linked God's specific blessing to a personal quality. Those of good will are blessed by God's peace. The angel added directions for finding the child, telling the men to look for a child "lying in a manger" (2:12).

The shepherds were men of action. When the angel left, they also hurried on their way to Bethlehem. They found the baby and his parents.

You will see the nativity scene, including the shepherds, everywhere during the Christmas season. When you do, imagine what must have gone through the minds of those shepherds. Too, remember that when they left the Child they did not immediately return to their flocks but spread the good news. We could say they were the first evange-lists (after the angels). Perhaps the town was waking to a new day, and the shepherds ran to their homes to tell their families and neighbors what had happened.

Mary absorbed all these events. She must have had a thoughtful nature and kept marveling at all that had hap-pened. She would have wondered what else lay ahead.

Implications and Actions

1. At Christmas, we see manger scenes in many places—in homes, in churches, on Christmas cards,

in stores. Central to the scene is the baby and his parents. They remind us of the importance of the home, rooted in creation and the first institution invented by God. Anything we do as a family or a church to strengthen our homes is right on target. God entrusted his only Son to a human home, thus underlining the home's sacredness.

2. From first to last, the Bible repeats that worship is for everyone. Shepherds and those who owned the sheep or who owned or ruled the land could receive God's blessing. God's Messiah was born to a working-class couple and announced first to men at work. Jesus came for you, whoever you are.

3. The Son of God was also fully human. He shared our life completely from the trauma of birth to the experience of death. The Gospels show him as experiencing a complete life from growing up to learning a trade, from making close friendships to facing opposition. Although God may seem at times far away, we can remember that Jesus has been here and he understands.

SAVIOR

In the Old Testament, God is Savior, delivering his people from slavery in Egypt and captivity in Babylon. In the New

Testament, God continues as Savior through his Messiah and Son. Jesus also becomes Savior, not only of Israel, but of the whole world—all who believe in him. The word *savior* can also mean *healer* and usually includes healing of the whole body and the whole self, not merely a part.

CHRIST

Christ is the Greek translation of the Hebrew word *Messiah*. Both words mean *anointed*. In the Old Testament, the word applies primarily to kings and sometimes priests. In the later Old Testament books, *Messiah* refers to God's anointed deliverer who will sit on the throne of David and deliver Israel. The Jewish mind of Jesus' day thought of military victories and kingship. Part of Jesus' task was teaching his followers that he was sent to deliver them from sin to righteousness. From constant use, *Christ* moved from being a title to another name for Jesus.

THE LORD

The title *lord* can mean simply *sir* or can refer to God. Its background is rooted in the idea of *one who has power and authority*. The Jews would not speak the name of God (*YHWH* or *Yahweh*), but instead substituted the Hebrew word *adonai* or *Lord*. The angel speaking to the shepherds certainly used the word *Lord* to point to Jesus' divinity.

QUESTIONS

1. What can you do to keep Christ in Christmas for yourself and your family? Be specific.

2. Remembering that God entrusted his Son to a human family, what can you do to make sure the children or grandchildren in your life experience deep human and divine love?

3. How are you responding today to the coming of the Savior, who is God's Messiah and Son?

NOTES

1. See Luke 8:19–21; Matthew 12:46–47; 13:55; John 2:12; 7:3, 5; Acts 1:14; 1 Corinthians 9:5; Galatians 1:19.

2. See, for example, Genesis 16:9, 11; 22:11.

LESSON FOUR

Committed to God's Purpose

MAIN IDEA

Jesus' childhood experience in the temple shows his commitment to God's purpose and calls us to consider our own commitment to God's purpose.

QUESTION TO EXPLORE

How committed are you to fulfilling God's purpose for your life?

STUDY AIM

To explain the significance of Jesus' experience in the temple at age twelve and to evaluate what your life indicates about your commitment to God's purpose

QUICK READ

When Jesus was twelve years old, he went to the temple with his parents. On the way home they could not find Jesus. They found him in the temple listening to and inquiring of the learned teachers.

When one of my sons was about six years old, he got lost. I expected him to show up at church after school for missions' organizations. When he didn't appear, I grew concerned. One of the arriving leaders told me she saw him walking downtown, but he had refused a ride. (He had learned *something*!)

I got in the car and went looking for him. Sure enough I found him trudging along trying to find the church. Poor guy! He had missed the bus for some reason, and although the church was only a couple of blocks away, he somehow went down the wrong street. I suspect most parents have at least one story like that. Jesus' parents certainly did.

LUKE 2:39–52

³⁹ When Joseph and Mary had done everything required by the Law of the Lord, they returned to Galilee to their own town of Nazareth. ⁴⁰ And the child grew and became strong; he was filled with wisdom, and the grace of God was upon him.

⁴¹ Every year his parents went to Jerusalem for the Feast of the Passover. ⁴² When he was twelve years old, they went up to the Feast, according to the custom. ⁴³ After the Feast was over, while his parents were returning home, the boy Jesus stayed behind in Jerusalem, but they were unaware of it. ⁴⁴ Thinking he was in their company, they

traveled on for a day. Then they began looking for him among their relatives and friends. **45** When they did not find him, they went back to Jerusalem to look for him. **46** After three days they found him in the temple courts, sitting among the teachers, listening to them and asking them questions. **47** Everyone who heard him was amazed at his understanding and his answers. **48** When his parents saw him, they were astonished. His mother said to him, "Son, why have you treated us like this? Your father and I have been anxiously searching for you."

49 "Why were you searching for me?" he asked. "Didn't you know I had to be in my Father's house?" **50** But they did not understand what he was saying to them.

51 Then he went down to Nazareth with them and was obedient to them. But his mother treasured all these things in her heart. **52** And Jesus grew in wisdom and stature, and in favor with God and men.

Background Passage: Jesus' First Temple Visit (2:21–38)

The Gospel of Luke frequently emphasizes the loyalty of Mary and Joseph to the observance of the law. Thus, Mary and Joseph carried Jesus to Jerusalem when he was eight days old, to be circumcised ritually in the temple.

On approaching the temple, the family successively met two elderly people, Simeon and Anna. Simeon was filled with the Holy Spirit, who had promised him he would not die before he saw the Messiah. On seeing Jesus, Simeon took him in his arms and gave thanks to God for allowing him to live to see such a child as this. Then the eighty-four-year-old Anna, known as a prophetess, also took the child, blessed him, and began to tell others about the one she had seen.

A Growing Boy (2:39–40)

After the circumcision, the little family returned to Nazareth for a more normal life. There Jesus grew to adulthood. He began to learn the carpentry trade with his earthly father. In the local synagogue, Jesus studied the Old Testament law. He also played in the streets and fields as any child might.

The Gospel of Luke comments that in Jesus' home at Nazareth, he grew strong. Physically, Jesus may have helped his father even before he was old enough to become an apprentice carpenter. Likely he ran and played vigorously, as most boys do.

Jesus also grew in wisdom. Although Jesus was the Son of God, he "emptied himself" (Philippians 2:7, NASB) to become human. Have you ever wondered whether Jesus had as hard a time as some of us do learning math or some other subject? He certainly studied the Old Testament carefully. As an adult, he quoted it freely and easily. But the word *wisdom* implies understanding and discernment beyond merely being acquainted with it. Perhaps he spent hours digesting and pondering its meaning.

Luke 2:40 is the first of two gaps in Jesus' life. The verse summarizes some twelve years. After the next story, there's a gap of perhaps eighteen years before Jesus began his ministry. But notice again that Jesus was increasing in wisdom. He would show that wisdom as he listened to and questioned the nation's religious leaders in the Jerusalem temple.

Another Temple Visit (2:41–52)

Mary and Joseph were a pious couple who apparently went to the temple for the feast of the Passover as often as they could. So when Jesus was age twelve, they took him on the eighty-five mile trip, which would have required several days. This feast marked the Exodus from Egypt by the Israelite people. The Exodus was God's great saving act in the Old Testament. Some psalms celebrate this great victory over the strongest nation on earth at the time. (See, for example, Psalm 78:12–55; 106:7–33.) *Passover* refers to the death angel's passing over each household that had sacrificed a lamb and splashed its blood over their door as God commanded. Those without the blood lost their firstborn son that night. As the last of the ten plagues, this terrible event led to Egypt's allowing the Israelites under Moses to go free. So, Passover was the major feast of the year, rich in history and celebrated by huge crowds from all over the world. Every male Jew was supposed to go to Jerusalem every year possible for this feast. Even today Jews all over the world who celebrate Passover in their homes include the hope and pledge *next year in Jerusalem.*

After the feast, the families packed their supplies and hit the roads on their way home. Mary and Joseph went a whole day's journey (about fifteen miles) before they began looking for Jesus. They had assumed he was in the crowd, along with his friends or cousins. But when they inquired, no one had seen him. At this point, some Bible commentators discuss what the parents did wrong and how they could have avoided this. I sometimes wonder whether those who make such comments have raised children. Young boys have a way of disappearing no matter how close you think you're watching them! Jesus *disappeared* in a different way. He had gone to school!

When Jesus' parents found him at last, he was still in the temple. He had found a group of teachers and was listening to them and asking them questions. Many have tried to picture this boy teaching these Jewish leaders. But the Scripture merely says he was listening and questioning, perhaps about God's activity through Moses and the Exodus. From Jesus' penetrating questions, the priests and rabbis could tell this lad was special in his intelligence and religious devotion. Jesus was even then laying the foundation for what he would teach twenty years later.

Jesus' parents were frantic and showed it. Their relief and exasperation spilled over as they told the boy they had been looking everywhere for him. They had been out of their minds with worry. Jesus, however, had been focused on only one thing. He pointed out they should have known what he was doing. The King James Version reads "about my father's business," and the New International Version says "in my father's house" (2:49). Literally, Luke wrote *in the things of my father.* So either *business* or *house* would be a possible translation.

Luke 2:51 is the highlight of the story. Jesus showed he already had a consciousness of being on mission for God. Although Jesus gave respect to his earthly father, he was clear that God was his true father. Jesus showed he was committed to the work God had called him to do.

Jesus was on the verge of adulthood. The story tells us that Jesus approached adulthood with a deep commitment to the mission God had given him.

Nevertheless, Jesus left the temple with his parents and returned to Nazareth. The Bible says Jesus was obedient to his parents. We might well reason for today's children that if Jesus could respect his parents, so can we.

Not for the first time, Luke tells us that Mary remembered these events and sayings and reflected on them (2:51; see 2:19). Again the Bible says that Jesus continued to grow in wisdom and stature, and that he was approved by both people and God. This is the only biblical story of Jesus' childhood. The story tells us that as a child, Jesus was already obeying God and seeking God's will.

Implications and Actions

1. Even from a young age, Jesus was committed to God's purpose. The rest of his life, especially the three years of public ministry, was devoted to carrying out that purpose. I experienced God's claim on my life at the age of eleven. That purpose has driven my life since then. I've had doubts of many things and strayed from time to time, but central to my life is the knowledge of the work God has called me to do. Do you have that sense of purpose? God calls not only those in church vocations but all Christians. He has a plan for your life, and life goes best when you find and follow it.

2. Another claim on your life as a Christian is serving God through God's church. From eight days old until the end of his life, Jesus was active in the temple and synagogue. You can have a sense of purpose in serving God through his church. Some of the most important things you do in life may be done in God's church.

3. Children make life-changing decisions through the church's ministry. In the church, children learn of God and Christ. They then are baptized, and they begin to grow as Christians. We must constantly reaffirm that we are seeking to develop mature followers of Christ. What we do in leading children is arguably the most important thing we do.

4. We should also recognize the importance Scripture gives to family life. Lesson three mentioned the manger scene as a depiction of family. Now we see Jesus' earthly parents taking him to the temple and helping him grow into adulthood. Jesus contributed to his earthly family by honoring and obeying his parents.

PLACES OF JESUS' LIFE

Bethlehem. Bethlehem is the village from which David came. Jesus was born there, emphasizing his relationship to the great king. The Jews expected a Messiah from among David's descendants.

Jerusalem. It's almost impossible for non-Jews to understand the importance of this city in the minds of the Jews of Jesus' day and even ours. Traditionally, the temple was built over the burial place of Abraham, considered the founder of the faith and the father of Israel. The temple and its inner sanctum, the holy of holies, was considered the closest one could come to God on earth. There the great sacrifices were made to atone for sins, and there the people held the great festivals, such as the one in this lesson.

Nazareth. This place was a small village. A few miles north was a much larger Roman town called Sepphoris. Jesus probably knew both Sepphoris and Capernaum, but he was raised in a small farming village. He played in its streets and fields. He was educated in its synagogue. He must have known everyone, and they knew him.

FINDING GOD'S WILL

- What abilities or talents has God given you?

- What interests has God given you?

- What are your major areas of concern? in your community? in the world?

- What doors do you see open? Is there a need at hand you can fill?

- Are you sensitive to the call of God?

QUESTIONS

1. What principle drives your life? Are you primarily concerned with raising a family, seeking success in business, or pleasing someone? Have you committed yourself to God's underlying purpose that can become the engine empowering and guiding your life?

2. What are some major experiences with God you have had? What were the results in your life?

3. Mary and Joseph took responsibility for bringing
   their son to the Lord's house. How much leadership
   in spiritual things do you show to your children or to
   children in your church and community?

4. How serious is your church about creating an
   environment for spiritual growth by children and
   youth?

UNIT TWO

Preparing for Ministry

After the exciting story of Jesus' birth, the Gospel of Luke fast forwards through most of Jesus' boyhood, picking up the story with John's ministry. This unit's lessons focus on a season of preparation. John's ministry helped prepare the people for Jesus' coming. It was also a time for Jesus to prepare. Through Jesus' baptism and temptation, he confirmed his commitment to God's plan and was empowered by the Holy Spirit for the intense three years of his public ministry.

Joy is woven throughout these lessons. In "Are You Ready for This?" (Luke 3:1–14), John's message calls us to repent and experience the joy of a renewed relationship with God. "Who's the Greatest?" (Luke 3:15–23a) reminds us of the joy that comes in giving Christ our full commitment. "When Temptation Comes" (Luke 4:1–13) anticipates the joyful news of Jesus' victory over sin and death and reminds us that Jesus' example gives us a pattern to follow when we experience temptation.

My study of Luke prompted me to examine my commitment to Christ. Have I really prepared myself for God to do all he wants to in and through me? I hope your study helps you prepare for God's work in your life as well.[1]

UNIT TWO: PREPARING FOR MINISTRY

Lesson 5	Are You Ready for This?	Luke 3:1–14
Lesson 6	Who's the Greatest?	Luke 3:15–23a
Lesson 7	When Temptation Comes	Luke 4:1–13

NOTES

1. All Scripture quotations in unit 2, lessons 5–7, are from the New American Standard Bible.

LESSON FIVE

Are You Ready for This?

MAIN IDEA

Entering into a genuine relationship
with God calls for turning
from unethical behavior.

QUESTION TO EXPLORE

Is repentance really necessary
for someone like me?

STUDY AIM

To identify ways in which I
need to enter into a genuine
relationship with God by turning
from unethical behavior

QUICK READ

John proclaimed to his listeners
that they needed to repent to ready
themselves for the coming Lord.
As with those original hearers,
repentance allows us to enter into
genuine relationship with God
and prepares the way for God
to work in and through us.

In his autobiography *Born Again*, Charles Colson told the story of how he realized he needed to repent. A top aide to President Richard Nixon, Colson was implicated as one of the conspirators in the Watergate break-in in 1972.

In the midst of the turmoil, Colson met with Tom Phillips, then president of Raytheon. Phillips had recently accepted Christ as his Savior. Intrigued by the change he saw in Phillips, Colson sought him out. Phillips shared the gospel with him and read to him from C.S Lewis's *Mere Christianity*. Confronted by the gospel, Colson recognized himself as a prideful and arrogant man. Colson shared how earlier in his life he had been unable to admit mistakes or failure. He took great pride in his reputation as Nixon's *hatchet man* and had spent his life jockeying for status and position. Repentance was necessary. Sometime after that conversation, Colson chose to follow Jesus as Lord.

Colson's change of heart was demonstrated by a change of action. He moved from denying any wrongdoing to entering a guilty plea. He eventually was indicted and served a prison term for his role in Watergate. After his release, Colson became the founder of Prison Fellowship. Prison Fellowship ministers to prisoners and their families through a network of volunteers who work in the prisons and through programs such as Angel Tree.[1]

Colson demonstrated his repentance by his changed behavior. Similarly, John the Baptist challenged his listeners to repent and turn from their unethical behavior.

We also must turn from our unethical behavior to have a genuine relationship with God.

LUKE 3:1–14

[1] Now in the fifteenth year of the reign of Tiberius Caesar, when Pontius Pilate was governor of Judea, and Herod was tetrarch of Galilee, and his brother Philip was tetrarch of the region of Ituraea and Trachonitis, and Lysanias was tetrarch of Abilene, [2] in the high priesthood of Annas and Caiaphas, the word of God came to John, the son of Zacharias, in the wilderness. [3] And he came into all the district around the Jordan, preaching a baptism of repentance for the forgiveness of sins; [4] as it is written in the book of the words of Isaiah the prophet, "The voice of one crying in the wilderness, 'Make ready the way of the Lord, Make His paths straight. [5] 'Every ravine will be filled, And every mountain and hill will be brought low; The crooked will become straight, And the rough roads smooth; [6] And all flesh will see the salvation of God.'" [7] So he began saying to the crowds who were going out to be baptized by him, "You brood of vipers, who warned you to flee from the wrath to come? [8] "Therefore bear fruits in keeping with repentance, and do not begin to say to yourselves, 'We have Abraham for our father,' for I say to you that from these stones God is able to raise up children to Abraham. [9] "Indeed the axe is already laid at the root of

the trees; so every tree that does not bear good fruit is cut down and thrown into the fire." **10** And the crowds were questioning him, saying, "Then what shall we do?" **11** And he would answer and say to them, "The man who has two tunics is to share with him who has none; and he who has food is to do likewise." **12** And some tax collectors also came to be baptized, and they said to him, "Teacher, what shall we do?" **13** And he said to them, "Collect no more than what you have been ordered to." **14** Some soldiers were questioning him, saying, "And what about us, what shall we do?" And he said to them, "Do not take money from anyone by force, or accuse anyone falsely, and be content with your wages."

God Speaks (3:1–2)

Luke began the story of John's ministry with a list of several political and religious leaders. His list included some figures who played important roles in the story of Jesus' life. Jesus appeared before Pontius Pilate and Herod as well as Jewish high priests Annas and Caiaphas during his trial (Luke 23:1–25; John 18:13, 24).

In addition to dating John's ministry, Luke's list of leaders had two other functions. This list of local, national, religious, and political leaders underscored one of Luke's major themes: Jesus came to bring salvation for all people. By including the emperor, Tiberius Caesar, Luke anticipated the story he would complete in Acts of how the gospel spread, even to Rome.

Luke's list of leaders also helped identify John as a prophet. The Old Testament introduces many prophets by dating their ministry in terms of who was in power at the time. Luke's statement in verse 2 that "the word of God came to John, son of Zacharias" echoes this Old Testament formula (see Jeremiah 1:1–3; Hosea 1:1; Zechariah 1:1 for examples).

Old Testament prophets told the people how God was working and called them to repent and renew their relationships with God. In his role as "forerunner" of the Messiah (Luke 1:17), John had the special function of going "on before the Lord to prepare his ways" (1:76). John's task was to call the people to repent and to prepare them for what God was about to do in the coming of Jesus, the Messiah.

Get Ready (3:3–6)

John began his ministry around the Jordan River by "preaching a baptism of repentance for the forgiveness of sins" (3:3). John elaborated on his message in verses 7–14.

Biblical repentance involves a change of mind and action. When we repent, we stop making excuses for ourselves and agree that what we have done is wrong in God's sight. Repentance is a choice to reject sin and turn toward

God. John made clear that he was calling for repentance that led to changed behavior, not merely to feel sorrow and regret.

The Greek word for "baptism" means *to dip or immerse*. The Jews practiced a form of baptism, but John's baptism was unique in Jewish culture. In the Old Testament, ceremonial cleansing and washing symbolized the removal of sin and uncleanness (Leviticus 16:4, 24). Later Jewish writings describe the baptism of converts to Judaism as an initiation rite, although this might not have been practiced during John's time. John urged his listeners to be baptized as a symbol of the commitment that had taken place. Forgiveness is found not in the act of baptism but in having an humble and repentant heart before God.

In the rural area near where my family lives are many dirt roads. After a rain, road crews use heavy equipment to smooth and level the roads for driving. Luke quoted from Isaiah 40, which describes the ancient process of smoothing and leveling roads for a king, specifically the preparation for the Lord's coming as he brought the people of Judah back from Exile. Verses 4–6 are a call to prepare for God's coming in the person of Jesus Christ. God was at work preparing a path for salvation to spread around the world.

The images in verse 5 of valleys being filled and mountains being made low anticipate the great reversal brought by Jesus' ministry. By sending his Son, God was doing something that would change the world forever.

Jesus chose not the proud and powerful but those who had humble and repentant hearts. When God is ready to work, God calls us to join him. Repentance is one way in which we prepare ourselves for what God is going to do.

God convicts us of sin so that we can be restored to right relationship with him. Repentance is our response to what God is doing in our hearts. Repentance removes the barriers sin erects between us and God. Psalm 66:18 says, "If I regard wickedness in my heart, the Lord will not hear." In 1 Peter 3:7, Peter exhorted husbands to treat their wives with understanding and honor "so that your prayers will not be hindered." Sin gets in the way of our relationship with God. When we reject our sinful behavior and ask God's forgiveness, God cleanses us and removes those obstacles. Repentance results in a renewed relationship with God.

Verse 6 says, "All flesh will see the salvation of God." Throughout the Gospel of Luke and its sequel, Acts, Luke made clear that the gospel is meant for all people. No one is excluded from the promise of salvation. The Old Testament is filled with dramatic examples of how God works when his people repent and restore their relationships with him. The revivals under Hezekiah (2 Chronicles 30—31) and Nehemiah (Nehemiah 8—9) are only two examples. History also teaches that great periods of revival begin when God's people repent. God moves in dramatic ways when his people are in right relationship with him.

God Is Near (3:7–14)

Repentance requires both a change of heart and a change of action. John admonished the crowds to prove the sincerity of their hearts by their actions. John compared the crowds to snakes fleeing a brush fire: "You brood of vipers, who warned you to flee from the wrath to come?" (Luke 3:7). John was challenging his listeners' motives: "Therefore bear fruits in keeping with repentance and do not begin to say to yourselves, 'We have Abraham for our father'" (3:8). Many Jews believed their status as children of Abraham made them right with God. John taught that one's heritage was not enough. Repentance is necessary for a true relationship with God. By calling the crowd *snakes*, John implied that their lack of repentance showed their true father was not Abraham but Satan. John's words may seem harsh, but when God convicts us of sin he does so because he loves us. God desires that we to turn from sin's destructive power to God's salvation.

John gave his hearers another reason to repent—the time of God's judgment was near. Jesus' coming brought salvation, but it also brought judgment for those who rejected his word. The images of the axe and of fire are used to describe judgment in the Old Testament (Genesis 19:24; Isaiah 10:34). John challenged the crowd to "bear fruit," or demonstrate their repentance with action. The time of judgment was at hand. The axe had already been laid at the root of the trees, ready to cut down those that did not bear fruit. In the same way, those who did not repent would face God's judgment.

The crowd's question, "Then what shall we do?" (Luke 3:10), showed that they had taken John's words to heart. When we repent, God changes us so that we desire to do what is right. John's answer showed another truth about repentance. Repentance is demonstrated in action, but it is also demonstrated in relationship.

Acts of generosity and compassion are two proofs of a changed heart. John told the crowd that "the man who has two tunics is to share with him who has none, and he who has food is to do likewise" (3:11). When God prompts us to share his blessings and we refuse, that is sin. A repentant heart is proved by our treatment of others.

The need to prove the genuineness of repentance is highlighted again in John's interaction with the tax collectors and soldiers (3:12–13). John instructed the tax collectors to collect no more than what they were ordered to collect. In the Roman Empire, the right to collect taxes was sold to various individuals. Tax collectors could collect a fee for personal compensation in addition to what was owed the government. Because those additional fees were not dictated by law, the system was rampant with abuse. Many tax collectors claimed exorbitant sums. Because of their abuse of power, tax collectors were hated and looked down on by the Jewish people. We demonstrate repentance by refusing to take advantage of or exploit others.

The soldiers who asked John "what shall we do?" were likely not Roman soldiers but Jewish troops serving under Herod Agrippa. They may have been assigned to protect and assist the tax collectors. Like the tax collectors, John told these soldiers not to abuse their power through extortion or bullying. Instead, he charged them to be content with their wages.

Wrong desires lead to wrong actions. Repentance also means rejecting desires such as greed that lead us to immoral behavior.

John charged his listeners to repent from sins of omission as well as commission. Abuse of power is a sin, but so are hard-heartedness and lack of compassion. We sin not only when we do something we know is wrong but also when we refuse do that which we know is right (James 4:17). Both active and passive sins require repentance before God.

Implications and Actions

Repentance is necessary for a genuine relationship with God. Repentance, however, is seldom easy. Sometimes pride gets in the way, and we make the mistake of thinking we don't need to repent. Hard-heartedness, selfishness, and lack of compassion are sins just as much as embezzlement, bribery, and abuse of power. True repentance is demonstrated in changes in both attitude and action.

BERTHA SMITH AND THE SHANTUNG REVIVAL

Bertha Smith served as a missionary in China's Shantung province in the early 1900s. The mission was characterized by spiritual apathy. Many of the Chinese Christians were considered *rice bowl* Christians, meaning they professed Christ out of a desire to gain something from the missionaries.

During a time of unrest, the missionaries retreated to the port city of Chefoo. While there they gathered in prayer. The wife of one of the missionaries was dramatically healed of an eye disease. Bertha was deeply convicted. The missionaries had spent a week repenting, and so they were spiritually prepared to pray for healing. However, they had never gone through such preparation to pray for the souls of the Chinese.

Revival began after many of the missionaries repented of unconfessed sin—broken relationships, jealousy, envy, and hatred. Then many people came to know Christ. In one school, all 600 girls and 900 out of 1000 boys accepted Christ. Repentance rejuvenated the missionaries' relationships with God and prepared the way for God to work.[2]

STEPS IN REPENTANCE:

1. Admit that you have sinned, and confess it to God. See what the Bible has to say about your sin. Refuse to make excuses or attempt to justify yourself any longer.

2. Recognize that sin has broken your relationship with God. Ask for God's forgiveness.

3. Change your actions. Ask God what changes you need to make to keep yourself from continuing in your old patterns. If you have hurt someone, make it right.

QUESTIONS

1. How does sin impact our relationships with others? with God?

2. Over whom do you have power or influence? How do you use that power?

3. Whom do you know who has a physical or spiritual need? How could you use your resources to help meet that need?

4. In what areas of your life is sin hindering your relationship with God?

5. Think of a time when God convicted you of sin and you repented. What changes did your repentance produce in your life?

NOTES ————————————————————————

1. Charles Colson, *Born Again* (Grand Rapids: Fleming, 1995), 92–93, 107–117, 130.

2. Bertha Smith, *Go Home and Tell* (Nashville: Broadman and Holman, 1995), 8, 35–50; C.L Culpepper, *The Shantung Revival* (Dallas: Evangelism Commission, BGCT, no date), 36–43.

FOCAL TEXT
Luke 3:15–23a

BACKGROUND
Luke 3:15–23a

LESSON SIX

Who's the Greatest?

MAIN IDEA

John's message and Jesus' baptism show how Jesus fulfilled God's magnificent purpose and call us to commitment to Jesus' Lordship.

QUESTION TO EXPLORE

In what way do you recognize Jesus as being worthy of your full commitment?

STUDY AIM

To describe how John's message and Jesus' baptism fulfilled God's purpose and to express my commitment to Jesus' Lordship

QUICK READ

John's message and Jesus' baptism challenge us in our commitment to Jesus' Lordship.

On March 15, 2004, Carrie McDonnall was the sole survivor of a drive-by shooting in Iraq that killed her husband, David, and three other Baptist workers. Well aware of the dangers, the McDonnalls had gone to Iraq in response to a strong sense of God's call. Their love for God and for the Iraqi people compelled them to go.

After the attack, Carrie said we should not shirk away from serving in the dangerous places. According to Carrie, if Jesus could suffer for us to the point of death on the cross, how can we not be willing to go to the hard and dangerous places for him? She and David went to Iraq not because someone sent them, but because God asked them to go.[1]

Stories like the McDonnall's challenge me in my commitment to Jesus. Sometimes God asks of me things I want to say are too hard. In this lesson, John recognized that Jesus was worthy of John's full commitment. How do I show Jesus is worthy of my full commitment? How do you?

LUKE 3:15–23A

[15] Now while the people were in a state of expectation and all were wondering in their hearts about John, as to whether he was the Christ, [16] John answered and said to them all, "As for me, I baptize you with water; but One is coming who is mightier than I, and I am not fit to untie the thong of His sandals; He will baptize you with the Holy Spirit

and fire. **17** "His winnowing fork is in His hand to thoroughly clear His threshing floor, and to gather the wheat into His barn; but He will burn up the chaff with unquenchable fire." **18** So with many other exhortations he preached the gospel to the people. **19** But when Herod the tetrarch was reprimanded by him because of Herodias, his brother's wife, and because of all the wicked things which Herod had done, **20** Herod also added this to them all: he locked John up in prison. **21** Now when all the people were baptized, Jesus was also baptized, and while He was praying, heaven was opened, **22** and the Holy Spirit descended upon Him in bodily form like a dove, and a voice came out of heaven, "You are My beloved Son, in You I am well-pleased." **23** When He began His ministry, Jesus Himself was about thirty years of age. . . .

One Who Is Greater Than I (3:15–18)

The Roman Empire dominated Palestine in the time of Jesus' ministry. Under the iron fist of Roman rule, the people's expectations of a deliverer, a messiah, became especially intense. Although most expected a deliverer to emerge from the descendants of King David, the Jews had differing understandings of the nature of that deliverance. Many expected the messiah would overthrow Rome and reestablish Jewish sovereignty. Others expected a priest who would restore and purify Israel's worship. The expectation of a "prophet like Moses" (Deuteronomy 18:15) was also linked to the idea of messiah. Some believed the messiah would usher in an age of prosperity and plenty.

With the various expectations in mind, it is easy to understand why the crowds wondered "in their hearts" whether John could be the Christ. "Christ" is the Greek translation of the Hebrew word *messiah*. John quickly set the crowds straight. John was not the Messiah, but the "forerunner," the one sent to prepare the way for the Messiah's coming (Malachi 3:1; 4:5–6).

John said the coming Messiah would be "greater" than he. In fact, John said, "I am not fit to untie the thong of His sandals" (Luke 3:16). In that time, unfastening someone else's sandals was the work of a slave. In fact, the task was considered so humiliating that it was not to be assigned to a Hebrew slave.[2] In comparison to Jesus' Lordship, John did not consider himself worthy of even the most humble service.

John also recognized Jesus would have a greater ministry than his. John baptized with water, but Jesus would "baptize you with the Holy Spirit and fire" (3:16). John baptized his followers with water as a symbol of their commitment to God. Jesus' followers would receive the gift of the Holy Spirit because of their commitment to Christ.

In Acts 2, Luke told the dramatic story of the coming of the Holy Spirit. After Jesus' resurrection and prior to the ascension, Jesus instructed his followers to wait in Jerusalem until they received what the Father had

promised (Acts 1:4). On the day of Pentecost, the Holy
Spirit came with the sound of a great rushing wind and
"tongues of fire" that rested on the disciples (Acts 2:2–4).
The disciples were filled with and empowered by the Holy
Spirit. In the same way today, when we repent of our sins
and commit ourselves to follow Christ, we are filled with
and empowered by the Holy Spirit for life and ministry.

Fire is a symbol of purity but also a symbol of judgment. Jesus brings hope to those who follow him but
judgment to those who reject him. John used the familiar
image of a wheat harvest to explain this to his listeners
(Luke 3:17). After wheat was harvested, it was tossed into
the air to separate the heavy grain from the lighter chaff.
The chaff blew away and could burn with explosive force.
In the same way, Jesus' ministry divides people. Those
who place their trust in him are saved; those who do not,
face God's righteous judgment.

Commitment at All Costs (3:19–20)

Here Luke narrated the end of John's ministry. The events
described are out of order chronologically, but Luke followed this order because Jesus' ministry followed John's.

Luke said that John "reprimanded" Herod the tetrarch
"because of Herodias, his brother's wife" (3:19). This Herod
is Herod Antipas, son of Herod the Great. Herod the Great
was the king who was in power when Jesus was born. Herod

Antipas divorced his first wife in order to marry Herodias. Herodias was Herod's niece and also the wife of his brother, Phillip. Marrying one's brother's wife was against Jewish law (Leviticus 18:16, 20:21). John also rebuked Herod because of other "wicked things" Herod had done.

Herod responded by imprisoning John. Later Herod had John beheaded at Herodias's request (Luke 9:9; Mark 6:14–29).

When confronted with the truth, some accept it and repent. Others reject the truth and attack the messenger. Herod is an example of the latter. John could have backed down or chosen to soften his rebuke, but he did not. John kept his commitment to God even in the face of opposition.

Most of us do not face imprisonment when we stand for what is right, but we may face other forms of opposition. We may face pressure from friends who don't understand the decisions we make or intimidation from people who reject the gospel as irrelevant. Coworkers may call us judgmental or narrow-minded when we claim Jesus is the only way to salvation. Are we willing to keep our commitment to Christ even when it is tough?

Consecrated for Service (3:21–23a)

Luke began his account of Jesus' ministry with Jesus' baptism. Jesus came to John to be baptized. Jesus did not seek baptism as a sign of repentance from sin but rather as a public commitment of himself to the task before him. From this point on, Jesus placed himself on the path that led to the cross. At Jesus' baptism, "the Holy Spirit descended upon Him in bodily form like a dove" (3:22), indicating God's affirmation of Jesus and Jesus' ministry and preparing Jesus for the hardships ahead.

Luke's account of Jesus' baptism is unique in that it emphasizes prayer: "while He was praying, heaven was opened" (3:21). Throughout the Gospel of Luke, Luke made special note of the role prayer played in the life of Jesus (6:12; 9:18, 28; 22:25–46; 23:34–46). Prayer was an expression of Jesus' relationship with and dependence on the Father. For us as Jesus' followers, prayer is also an expression of our relationship with and dependence on God. Through prayer, we are empowered for service.

Luke says that the "Holy Spirit descended on Him in bodily form like a dove" (3:22). *Messiah* means *anointed one*. By anointing Jesus with the Holy Spirit, God publicly announced that Jesus was indeed the promised Messiah. Although nowhere in the Old Testament is the Holy Spirit depicted as a dove, early Christians recognized the dove as a symbol of the Holy Spirit. Jesus' anointing with the Holy Spirit was a fulfillment of Isaiah 61:1: "The Spirit of the Lord God is upon me." Jesus declared the fulfillment of this prophecy when he read it aloud in the synagogue at Nazareth (Luke 4:18).

In addition to the Spirit's anointing, God spoke from heaven: "You are My beloved Son, in You I am well-pleased" (3:22). God's words combine two Old Testament ideas. In Psalm 2:7, God announced the Messiah's reign by saying "You are My Son, Today I have begotten you." In Isaiah 42:1, God says that his chosen servant is "one in whom My soul delights." Jesus is both king and servant. By publicly proclaiming Jesus as Messiah, God announced that a new time had come.

Note some parallels between Jesus' anointing with the Holy Spirit at his baptism and the coming of the Holy Spirit at Pentecost. At his baptism, Jesus was anointed with the Spirit after prayer in preparation for ministry. At Pentecost, Jesus' followers received the Holy Spirit after prayer and were empowered for ministry. As followers of Christ, we are empowered by the Holy Spirit through prayer and our relationship with God. Our commitment to Christ should also lead us to Spirit-empowered service.

For us as believers today, baptism is a symbol of our commitment to Christ and the life change produced by that commitment. Being immersed in water symbolizes our death to sin and our old way of life; being raised up symbolizes our new life in Christ. Baptism is a public declaration that we have pledged our allegiance to God. Baptism has no power to save, but it is a powerful symbol of the commitment we have already made.

Implications and Actions

John recognized Jesus as being worthy of John's full commitment and kept that commitment in the face of persecution. Through his baptism, Jesus also demonstrated his commitment to God and the task God had called him to do.

We too must recognize Jesus as being worthy of our full commitment. Baptism is one way we demonstrate that commitment. At baptism we publicly announce that we have chosen to follow Christ. Our old way of life is gone forever; now we belong to God. We also demonstrate the commitment in a verbal witness to Christ and in a lifestyle that is obedient to him. If we say that Jesus is worthy of our full commitment, we must prove that in our actions as well.

FAITHFUL UNDER PERSECUTION: BAPTISTS IN ENGLAND (1660–68)

During the 1660s in England, the British parliament enacted a series of laws called the Clarendon Code that made it difficult for non-Anglican religious groups to meet. One of the most difficult restrictions for Baptists was an act that set penalties for unofficial worship services of more than five people.

English Baptists also faced public persecution. Families lived in fear of mobs, and some even had their children beaten by neighborhood gangs.

The laws did not prevent Baptist churches from meeting. Churches met in homes and set lookouts to warn the congregation if the authorities were approaching. Pastors were frequently imprisoned, only to begin preaching again as soon as they were released. One pastor, Benjamin Keach, was condemned to spend one day in the public stocks. He preached there, too.

Despite the persecution, few Baptists returned to the state church. In 1679, in the midst of the persecution, Baptists in Bristol founded Bristol Baptist College, still in existence today. It is the oldest Baptist college in the world.[3]

CASE STUDY

A young woman who has attended your church several times has some questions about baptism. She has accepted Christ and says that she attends church and reads her Bible regularly. However, she has never been baptized and isn't sure why baptism is important or necessary. What would you say?

QUESTIONS

1. How is your submission to Jesus' authority evident in your life?

2. Have you ever shared the truth with someone only to have them turn against you? How did you respond?

3. If you have been baptized, reflect on that experience. What did it mean to you at the time? How have you grown in your relationship with God since? If you have not been baptized, take a few moments to consider why. How have you publicly demonstrated your commitment to Christ?

4. Take a few moments to consider your commitment to Christ. Is there anything God has asked something of you that you have been unwilling to do? What do you need to do to make it right?

5. In what areas do you need to experience the power of the Holy Spirit for life or for ministry? Prayerfully ask God to empower you for doing his will.

NOTES

1. Lauri Arnold, "When God said 'I want you there,' McDonnalls went to Iraq," Baptist Press, http://www.baptistpress.com/bpnews. asp?id=18840, Accessed 3/10/09.

2. I. Howard Marshall, *The Gospel of Luke: A Commentary on the Greek Text* (William B. Eerdmans Publishing: Grand Rapids, 1978), 146.

3. H. Leon McBeth, *The Baptist Heritage* (Broadman Press: Nashville, 1987), 113–120.

FOCAL TEXT

Luke 4:1–13

BACKGROUND

Luke 4:1–13

LESSON SEVEN

When Temptation Comes

MAIN IDEA

Jesus' resistance to the temptations shows his faithfulness to God in every way and provides a model for our own faithfulness.

QUESTION TO EXPLORE

What help does Jesus' resistance to the temptations provide for you as you face your greatest temptation today?

TEACHING AIM

To tell how the meaning of Jesus' temptations applies to my experiences with temptation today

QUICK READ

Jesus' demonstration of faithfulness in the face of his temptations in the wilderness provides a model for me to follow in my struggle against sin and temptation.

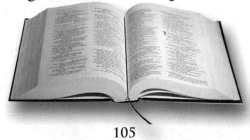

Sometimes my daily battle against temptation begins before I even get out of bed. What harm could it do to hit the snooze one more time? Does it really matter whether my quiet time gets cut a little short or skipped altogether? Then there are those moment by moment choices. Do I indulge in a juicy piece of gossip or end the conversation? Do I give in to my critical spirit or redirect my thoughts?

Some temptations no one else sees—those that take place between my head and my heart. Where do I find the strength to respond with grace to my children instead of losing patience? How do I bite back my sarcastic words instead of speaking them to my husband? How do I motivate myself to use my time productively instead of wasting time on the Internet?

I sometimes win the battle, but I fail more often than I would like to admit. Knowing that Jesus was tempted and overcame temptation gives me hope. I serve a God who understands my weaknesses and provides me a way of escape when temptation comes. Jesus' victory over temptation encourages me because his life gives me a pattern to follow in my moments of weakness.

LUKE 4:1–13

[1] Jesus , full of the Holy Spirit, returned from the Jordan and was led around by the Spirit in the wilderness [2] for forty days, being tempted by the devil. And He ate

nothing during those days, and when they had ended, He became hungry. **3** And the devil said to Him, "If You are the Son of God, tell this stone to become bread." **4** And Jesus answered him, "It is written, 'Man shall not live on bread alone.'" **5** And he led Him up and showed Him all the kingdoms of the world in a moment of time. **6** And the devil said to Him, "I will give You all this domain and its glory; for it has been handed over to me, and I give it to whomever I wish. **7** "Therefore if You worship before me, it shall all be Yours." **8** Jesus answered him, "It is written, 'You shall worship the Lord your God and serve Him only.'" **9** And he led Him to Jerusalem and had Him stand on the pinnacle of the temple, and said to Him, "If You are the Son of God, throw Yourself down from here; **10** for it is written, 'He will command His angels concerning You to guard You,' **11** and, 'On their hands they will bear You up, So that You will not strike Your foot against a stone.'" **12** And Jesus answered and said to him, "It is said, 'You shall not put the Lord your God to the test.'" **13** When the devil had finished every temptation, he left Him until an opportune time.

Depending on God Alone (4:1–4)

After the narrative of Jesus' baptism, Luke included Jesus' genealogy. Luke traced Jesus' family tree all the way back to Adam (Luke 3:23–37). The genealogy establishes Jesus not only as a representative of Israel but also of all humanity, perhaps to contrast his response to temptation with that of Adam. When confronted with temptation, Adam sinned and was expelled from the garden. The people of Israel repeatedly turned their backs on God. Would Jesus be able to remain faithful in the face of temptation?

Jesus was both "full of the Holy Spirit" and "led around by the Spirit in the wilderness" (4:1). Jesus' relationship with God did not exempt him from temptation. Being filled with and led by the Holy Spirit doesn't make you immune to temptation; it makes you Satan's target. The Holy Spirit is not a shield from temptation but provides the power to overcome.

Luke said that the Holy Spirit led Jesus into the wilderness for forty days (4:2). The area west of the Jordan River between Jerusalem and Jericho was a barren wasteland and likely the location of Jesus' time of prayer and testing. His forty days in the wilderness recalls Israel's forty years of wandering in the wilderness (Numbers 14:26–35). Unlike Israel, Jesus was victorious in the face of temptation.

Satan attacked Jesus at a time of great weakness. Jesus had fasted during this forty-day period, and at the end of that time he "became hungry" (Luke 4:2). During a prolonged fast, most individuals stop feeling hunger pains only to have them return between twenty and forty days into the fast.[1] Satan came to Jesus when his hunger was strongest and his defenses were lowest.

Satan's words challenged Jesus' dependency on God: "If you are the Son of God, tell this stone to become bread"

(4:3). The Greek word translated "if" means *since.* Satan was challenging Jesus to prove his identity as the Messiah by using his power to provide food for himself rather than relying on God's provision. In addition to meeting his own needs, Jesus could easily have won crowds by supplying them with miraculous supplies of food. Satan was tempting Jesus to avoid the path of sacrifice and suffering.

Jesus responded by quoting Scripture: "It is written, 'Man shall not live by bread alone'" (4:4). Jesus was quoting from Deuteronomy 8:3, in which Moses explained to the people of Israel that God fed them with manna during the Exodus so they might learn to depend on him. Jesus reaffirmed his dependence on God. He would not take matters into his own hands. God supplied Jesus with both the physical and spiritual resources he needed to be obedient, even to the cross.

Resisting temptation often means saying no to ourselves. There are more important things than our own desires. Like Jesus, we can resist temptation when we depend on God to supply our needs. We depend on God not only for our physical needs, but also for the spiritual strength and endurance God supplies. When God calls us to do something, we should trust him to provide what is needed.

Having No Other gods (4:5–8)

The order of the temptations varies between Matthew and Luke. Matthew placed the temptation on the mountain last, but Luke placed it second in order to shift the climactic scene to the temple. In verse 5, Luke described a visionary experience in which the devil led Jesus to the top of a tall mountain and showed him "all the kingdoms of the world in a moment of time" (4:5). Satan claimed to have authority over the world and told Jesus that "if You worship before me, it shall all be Yours" (4:7).

There is some question whether Satan's claim was true. Although Satan is referred to as the "ruler of the world" (John 14:30), Scripture makes clear that Satan's authority is limited. In fact, Jesus clearly demonstrated his authority and power over Satan at every encounter (Luke 10:18; 11:14–23; 13:16; 22:31–32). Satan is, after all, the "father of lies" (John 8:44), and his promises at Jesus' temptation were either lies or gross exaggerations.

Satan's goal was obvious. Satan was not asking for a single moment of prayer but a full shift of allegiance. If Satan could successfully induce Jesus to worship him, this act would have ruptured the relationship between God the Father and God the Son. Such an act would have had cosmic consequences.

One problem with temptation is that it always looks good at the moment. Satan's promises glitter like gold but turn to dust in our hands. When we give in to temptation, sin may bring momentary pleasure, but the price is always too high for us to pay. Satan's goals for us are the same as they have always been: to break our relationship with God and lead us to destruction.

Again, Jesus responded with Scripture. He quoted Deuteronomy 6:13: "It is written, 'You shall worship the Lord your God and serve Him only'" (Luke 4:8). Jesus' absolute commitment was to worship and serve God alone. Jesus would receive all authority and power, but Jesus would wait to receive it directly from the hand of God. He refused any shortcuts that would direct him away from God's will and the way of the cross.

It looks clear-cut to us. Who among us would knowingly bow down in worship to Satan? However, anytime we allow something else to be more important than God we commit the same sin. Idolatry is idolatry, regardless of the object.

Sometimes the most subtle temptations are the ones that tempt us to settle for good over best. In our church lives today, we often settle for activity and a full calendar rather than a deep and personal relationship with God. Jesus was able to resist temptation because he knew God intimately. Cultivating our relationship with God helps us grow in our commitment to worship God alone.

Trusting, Not Testing (4:9–13)

After being rebuked twice with Scripture, Satan tried to twist Scripture to his own advantage. Satan led Jesus to the pinnacle of the temple and said: "If you are the Son of God, throw yourself down from here" (4:9). Satan was

quoting a messianic psalm (Psalm 91:11–12) that promises God's protection on his chosen one. As in verse 3, the
word "if" carries the force of *since*. Satan was again asking
Jesus to prove his status as Messiah. Part of the first-century messianic expectation was that the Messiah would do
wonders in the temple. People also expected wonder- or
miracle-workers to demonstrate divine protection. Satan
was tempting Jesus to cater to the people's expectations
and take a path to power other than the cross.

Jesus was not swayed by Satan's easy quotation of
Scripture. Jesus responded again with a quote from
Deuteronomy: "You shall not put the Lord your God to
the test" (Deut. 6:16). For Jesus to force God's hand in this
way would not have been a sign of faith, but of manipula-
tion and unbelief. Jesus had no need to ask God to prove
what Jesus already knew to be true.

How do we test God? There is a difference between a
genuine seeking after God and a demand that God prove
his existence or his character. The first is motivated by
humility and need, the second by skepticism and pride.
Israel tested God after escaping from Egypt. Despite
God's miraculous deliverance, they doubted God's ability
to provide for their needs and resorted to complaining.
Moses rebuked them for testing God (Exodus 17:1–7).
Ananias and Sapphira tested God when they lied about
bringing their full profit as a gift to the church. Their
deceit tested God's ability to judge, and they faced severe
consequences (Acts 5:1–10). We test God when we act as

if we are immune to God's judgment or demand that God prove what God has already shown to be true.

We must also be aware that Satan knows the Bible and can quote it for his purposes. Cult groups are famous for twisting Scripture and can easily snare those who do not have a solid foundation in the Scriptures. When studying the Bible, we should always consider the context of a particular verse. That is, we should also read the paragraph or two surrounding our particular verse to get a better sense of the meaning. It can also be helpful to use a concordance or topical reference to find what else the Bible has to say on the topic. Finally, we should always remember that the Holy Spirit is a great Teacher. We should pray and ask God to give us insight into Scripture.

After Jesus' rebuke, Satan left Jesus "until an opportune time" (Luke 4:13). This was not a one-time battle; Jesus faced temptation throughout his earthly life. Unlike us, though, Jesus was perfectly without sin. His sinless life allowed Jesus to become the perfect sacrifice for our sins. Satan was defeated at the cross. Jesus gives us the power to resist temptation and live victoriously in him.

Implications and Actions

Jesus' temptations remind me of two things. The first is Hebrews 4:15, which says that in Jesus "we do not have a high priest who cannot sympathize with our weaknesses, but One who has been tempted in all things as we are, yet without sin." Knowing that Jesus faced very real temptations gives me hope. Jesus sympathizes with our weaknesses because he walked through them victoriously.

The Bible also says God will not allow us to be tempted beyond what we can bear and that when we are tempted God is always faithful to provide a way of escape (1 Corinthians 10:13). I know that I will be tempted, but God's Word gives me the confidence that God will always provide a way out.

Jesus' example shows us some of those ways of escape. Depend on God alone. Refuse any substitutes for God's presence in your life. Know God and devote yourself to the study of God's word. Jesus' life, death, and resurrection give us the ultimate hope. Satan has been defeated once for all, and one day we will reign with Christ in victory.

WHAT THE BIBLE SAYS ABOUT TEMPTATION

Consider this brief survey of some of the Bible's teachings about temptation:

- God is not tempted, and God does not tempt anyone (James 1:13). God may test our loyalty to him as he did with Abraham (Genesis 22:1), but God does not tempt us to do evil.

- Temptation comes from both inside and outside sources. Some temptation comes from the great tempter, Satan (1 Thessalonians 3:5; Revelation 2:10). We can also be tempted and led astray by our own evil or selfish desires (James 1:14).

- We should be aware of our weaknesses and not think that we are above temptation (1 Cor. 10:12). We can pray and ask God to keep us away from temptation (Matthew 6:13) and to prevent us from falling into temptation through our own weakness (Mark 14:38).

- God always gives us a choice. In his grace, God does not allow us to be tempted beyond what we can bear and always provides a way out so that we can remain faithful (1 Cor. 10:13).

CASE STUDY

A young man from your church comes home from his first semester at college and shares some of his struggles with you. One of his professors is openly antagonistic to Christianity. One roommate keeps posters of swimsuit models on the wall and a stack of pornographic magazines next to the bed. The other roommate parties late on Saturday night and complains when the alarm goes off on Sunday morning. His friends often buy concert tickets and other expensive things he wants but can't afford. He wants to live a godly life, but it's hard. How can you encourage him?

QUESTIONS

1. How are you encouraged by knowing that Jesus was tempted and was able to resist temptation successfully? What can you learn from Jesus' example?

2. Satan likes to attack at our most vulnerable points. What are some areas in your life where you are most vulnerable to temptation? What can you do to become stronger in those areas?

3. What are some guidelines we can use to know when someone is using Scripture incorrectly?

4. What are some Scripture verses you find helpful in resisting temptation?

5. Think of a time when you successfully resisted
   temptation. What happened? What did you learn
   through that experience?

N O T E S ——————————————————————————

1. Richard Foster, *Celebration of Discipline* (San Francisco: Harper, 1988), 59.

UNIT THREE

Jesus' Ministry in Galilee

Unit three focuses on Jesus' ministry in Galilee. Lessons eight and nine explore the implications of Jesus' sermon at the synagogue in Nazareth. In lesson ten, we review the story of Jesus' call to Peter to gather people for Jesus' kingdom. Lesson eleven surveys Jesus' "Sermon on the Plain," and lesson twelve recounts Jesus' instruction to Simon the Pharisee about forgiveness and love.

Taken as a whole, the Scripture passages in this unit depict Jesus going against the grain of culture. He upset culturally conditioned expectations regarding the Messiah, marginalized people, and Gentiles.

Jesus challenges those who follow him to take up a new and life-defining task and to lay aside revenge in favor of intentional love. He insists that human estimates of righteousness and sinfulness be revised in light of our common need for God's forgiveness.[1]

UNIT THREE: JESUS' MINISTRY IN GALILEE

NOTES ───────────────────────────────────

1. Unless otherwise indicated, all Scripture translations in unit 3,
   lessons 8–12, are from the New Revised Standard Version.

LESSON EIGHT

Fulfilled Today?

MAIN IDEA

God's mission of justice as well as redemption has been fulfilled in Jesus, whom we are to follow.

QUESTION TO EXPLORE

To what extent are you and your church truly involved in God's mission of justice and redemption?

STUDY AIM

To evaluate whether and how I truly am involved in God's mission of justice and redemption fulfilled in Jesus

QUICK READ

Jesus declared himself the fulfillment of God's double-edged mission of justice and redemption. Jesus calls us to embrace him and his mission.

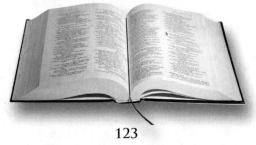

Have you ever thought you understood God's purpose only to discover you had missed a big piece of it? Such a thing may happen even in church.

For example, a missions speaker spoke in the morning service at my boyhood church. Short, slender, grey-haired, and stooped, he shared the story of his work among the poor in the Deep South. The congregation responded positively throughout most of his presentation. They liked it when he told them he shared the gospel with poor people. Our church members liked it even more when he told them some had become Christians, been baptized, and started a small church.

But the congregation stiffened when the missionary said he had learned a new thing from his work among the poor. He said,

> I've learned it's not enough to preach and teach and baptize. Many of the people I work with cannot get ahead because they are in poor health, never got to finish school, or face prejudice in the workplace. I've started working with anyone I can to find ways to help them get good health care, keep their children in school, and challenge prejudice. As you can imagine, I'm not too popular with some folk!

He smiled and laughed. The congregation sat dead silent. I could sense their unease, although I was too young to understand it. Now I do. The missionary challenged their understanding of what God would and would not do. They believed God wanted all people to hear the gospel, accept Jesus as Savior, and follow Jesus through baptism. On the other hand, they had never met anyone who believed God intended to change social structures. The visiting missionary, who had come to believe God joined justice and redemption in one mission, startled them. Many of them were not ready to accept that God combined justice and redemption into one mission for his church.

LUKE 4:14–21

14 Then Jesus, filled with the power of the Spirit, returned to Galilee, and a report about him spread through all the surrounding country. 15 He began to teach in their synagogues and was praised by everyone. 16 When he came to Nazareth, where he had been brought up, he went to the synagogue on the sabbath day, as was his custom. He stood up to read, 17 and the scroll of the prophet Isaiah was given to him. He unrolled the scroll and found the place where it was written: 18 "The Spirit of the Lord is upon me, because he has anointed me to bring good news to the poor. He has sent me to proclaim release to the captives and recovery of sight to the blind, to let the oppressed go free, 19 to proclaim the year of the Lord's favor." 20 And he rolled up the scroll, gave it back to the attendant, and sat

down. The eyes of all in the synagogue were fixed on him.
[21] Then he began to say to them, "Today this scripture has
been fulfilled in your hearing."

Filled With the Spirit (4:14)

Jesus returned from his fast and temptation experience in
the wilderness (see Luke 4:1–13, lesson 7). Filled with the
Spirit, Jesus took up his active ministry. He began in his
home territory, Galilee.

The phrase "filled with the power of the Spirit" merits
attention. Through it, Luke reminds us Jesus' mission was
framed, guided, and empowered by the same Spirit who
had worked through the ages to shape the world according to God's design. For example, the Spirit called each of
the prophets. Their prophetic message joined the themes
of redemption and justice. The phrase "filled with the
power of the Spirit" connects the prophets' message and
the lifework of Jesus.

Back Home in Nazareth (4:15–17)

The Gospel of Luke subtly reminds us Jesus was a first-
century Jew. It does so with a simple statement: "He
went to the synagogue on the sabbath day, as was his
custom." We naturally look at Jesus from the far end of

twenty centuries of Christian history. Let us remember, though, that Jesus spoke first as a Jew to his fellow Jews. If we want to understand Jesus better, we must discover the teachings, practices, and perceptions current in his day.

Synagogue worship followed a pattern. First came a call to worship, the *Shema* ("Hear, O Israel, the LORD our God is One"; see Deuteronomy 6:4). The worshipers might then recite the Ten Commandments plus other standard sayings. Portions of the Jewish Scriptures were read, some according to a set calendar of readings, others at the choice of the reader. Any man in good standing in the synagogue might be asked to read the Scriptures and offer an interpretation. The service concluded with a blessing.

As was customary, Jesus stood to read the Scriptures and sat to teach. Quite possibly, the congregation stood while he taught. In any case, the synagogue leader handed Jesus the scroll of Isaiah. Jesus found Isaiah 61:1–2 and read it aloud.

The Mission of God (4:18–19)

Jesus read Isaiah 61:1–2a. Centuries before, the words brought hope to the Jewish captives in Babylon that they might be set free and return to Jerusalem. In Jesus' time a segment of Judaism assumed the verses might refer to the work of the anticipated Messiah.

"The Spirit of the Lord is upon me, because he has anointed me." Isaiah spoke of God's Spirit calling him to take up God's mission. In similar fashion, God's Spirit worked in Jesus' baptism experience (Luke 3:21–22) and wilderness retreat (4:1–13). The mission Jesus announced in the synagogue at Nazareth was God's mission. Those who honor God and God's Messiah are called to embrace it.

". . . to bring good news to the poor." What does the term "poor" mean? Christians often rush to spiritualize the term to mean those who are humble before God, but Luke's Gospel takes a different tack. The "poor" were those on the low end of the economic ladder. Many were day laborers, people with no steady income who attempted to find work each day to provide basic food and shelter for their families. God's "good news" included an economic dimension. Jesus, drawing on Isaiah, aligned God with "the poor."

". . . to proclaim release to the captives." Isaiah announced God was about to free his people from the Babylonian captivity. God's redemption involved politics and economics. The phrase also carried political overtones in Jesus' time, especially to first-century Jews who lived under the rule of Rome. Isaiah's announcement also includes the idea of freedom from bondage to sin or to the penalty of sin. Jesus, like Isaiah, combined the two emphases.

". . . recovery of sight to the blind." Jesus' ministry included healing the blind. Such miracles literally liberated people from blindness. The miracles also linked Jesus' work to prophetic promises such as Isaiah 35:5 and

42:6–7. In Luke's Gospel, the healing of blindness included the idea of opening one's eyes to the light of God, enabling one to see the way of God more clearly.

"*. . . to let the oppressed go free.*" Isaiah portrayed the Jewish exiles in Babylon as oppressed, that is, held against their will in order to serve the political purposes of Babylon. The prophet promised God would act to end such oppression. The Jews would be freed from their captivity. Jesus took Isaiah's words and declared God was about to do the same kind of thing once again. Those who lived under political captivity would be set free as God's kingdom burst forth.

"*. . . to proclaim the year of the Lord's favor.*" Isaiah and Jesus referred to the *Year of Jubilee* as found in Leviticus 25. I never heard Leviticus 25 preached or taught while growing up in a small Baptist church. No wonder. Its vision is startling. Every fifty years the people of God were to erase all debts and return all property to its original owners. In short, all God's people would get a fresh economic start. Jesus tapped this tradition to stress that God's kingdom included a passion for economic justice.

A good friend of mine once asked me, "But what about salvation? I thought the passage was about redemption. Isn't God's primary mission to find, forgive, and save sinners? I never heard anyone talk about all this economic and political stuff!"

"Of course, the passage is about redemption," I responded. "It's just that redemption involves more than

I used to realize. The longer I've studied the background Old Testament passages, the more I've come to see God's kind of redemption is a package. It includes personal salvation and social justice—individual reconciliation with God and all kinds of reconciliation among people."

The Claim of Jesus (4:20–21)

Jesus sat down, assuming the traditional position of a teacher in that time. He made an astounding announcement: "Today this scripture has been fulfilled in your hearing." At the very least, Jesus proclaimed the promises of Isaiah had begun to come true in the moment he read the Scripture aloud. More likely, Jesus laid claim to be the living fulfillment of the promises. Jesus declared himself to be the promise and mission of God in the flesh.

The Lesson in Life

Our church tries to find ways to embrace God's mission. We invite people to accept personal salvation through faith in Christ. We also attempt to partner with God to be good news to the marginalized. Slowly we've discovered the two emphases mesh well.

For example, a few years ago we learned many families in our area with special needs children do not participate in church life. Eventually we established a ministry to special needs children and their families. The ministry included Sunday School, sports, social activities, life-skills classes, and art classes.

In order to launch the ministry, we had to change our perceptions and ways. We chose to free up programming time, space, and volunteers for the sake of the families and their children. We set aside our preconception of what such families needed. Instead, we sat down with parents and listened as they taught us about their life. They told us about their dreams, struggles, and needs. Together, we developed a vision for the ministry. Today the parents and the rest of us partner to provide the ministry. When I watch our special needs children, I almost feel as if I can see the *Year of Jubilee*, "the Year of the Lord's favor" (Luke 4:19), coming to pass for them.

SYNAGOGUE

Synagogues probably began during the Babylonian exile (about five hundred years before Christ). The temple in Jerusalem had been destroyed. The ancient people of God developed the synagogue as a place where they could meet to pray, reflect on Scripture, and preserve their way of life. By the time of Jesus, synagogues existed throughout the Roman Empire.

Prayers and Scripture readings were at the heart of synagogue worship. In the first century, the Pentateuch (the

first five books of the Hebrew Bible) was read each week.
The readings moved through a three-year cycle. Selections
from the prophets were also read aloud, although probably
not according to a set order of readings. The Scripture
readings were read aloud in Hebrew. The reader or
someone else might then translate the reading into a local
language, such as Aramaic. Exposition on the Scripture
readings seems to have been optional. The synagogue
leaders might invite any person, even a guest, to take up
the task.

The two most important synagogue officials were called
the *archisynagogos* and the *hazzan*. The *archisynagogos*, or
head of the synagogue, led the synagogue. We might think
of the office in terms of the synagogue's chief administrator.
The *hazzan* functioned as a key assistant to the head of the
synagogue.

APPLYING THE LESSON

Try the following exercises to help you apply the lesson:

- Ask God to plant his vision for ministry in your heart

- Research the spiritual, economic, and other needs of
  people who live within reach of your church

- Search out several other churches who have
  established ministries to marginalized people and
  interview those who work in those ministries

- Determine to be God's good news to a marginalized person or people group over the next twelve months. Make this an individual or a class project.

QUESTIONS

1. Thinking about the story of the missions speaker from the first paragraphs of the lesson comments, can you recall a time when something in a worship service led you to rethink your understanding of God's mission?

2. Do you think God's mission remains the same or changes over the centuries?

3. If we accept Jesus' contention that justice and redemption are intertwined in God's mission, how might the ministries of your class or church change? stay the same?

4. What people or people groups in your region might correspond to what Jesus meant by "the poor," "the captives," "the blind," and "the oppressed" (4:18)?

FOCAL TEXT

Luke 4:22–30

BACKGROUND

Luke 4:22–30

LESSON NINE

Jesus' Radical Message

MAIN IDEA

Jesus' ministry as Messiah is to all people, not just people like us.

QUESTION TO EXPLORE

What part of God's message do you, your class, or your church resist hearing?

STUDY AIM

To analyze whether my church and I have embraced Jesus' ministry to all people, not just people like us

QUICK READ

Jesus declared his ministry was to all kinds of people and called the people of God to follow his lead. Many resisted, and many of us still resist.

"How could you possibly believe God loves such people? I don't want anything to do with them!"

I remember thinking at that moment: "Why did I ever think I ought to become a pastor?" The small church called me to serve as their pastor about the time I turned nineteen years old. Six months into the pastorate, our mission leadership asked me to teach a missions study. The final session asked us to think about people in our community who might need to hear the gospel. The group generated several answers. Finally, someone mentioned people living in a local trailer park.

Everyone in the room knew about the trailer park. Twenty or so old trailers filled the lot. The poorest of the poor in our area lived there. They often stayed only a short time. Drug and alcohol abuse, domestic violence, malnourishment, and crime plagued the inhabitants. A few years before, another church had tried to include the children in the trailer park in Sunday School. The few children who came disrupted class, and the church soon abandoned the effort.

Still, someone in the group mentioned "the people in the trailer park" when we began to list those near us who might need the good news of Christ. A small woman seated on a back pew erupted and angrily said, "How could you possibly believe God loves such people? I don't want anything to do them!"

Stunned, I searched for the right words with which to respond. Fortunately for me, one of our deacons took the lead. He said, "Sounds to me as if the trailer-park folk are our Gentiles." After a moment, nearly everyone laughed gently. The group relaxed. The deacon's words reframed the discussion. He helped us start to challenge our tendency to limit God's ministry to people like us.

Similar dynamics came into play long ago on the day Jesus spoke in the synagogue in Nazareth.

LUKE 4:22–30

22 All spoke well of him and were amazed at the gracious words that came from his mouth. They said, "Is not this Joseph's son?" 23 He said to them, "Doubtless you will quote to me this proverb, 'Doctor, cure yourself!' And you will say, 'Do here also in your hometown the things that we have heard you did at Capernaum.'" 24 And he said, "Truly I tell you, no prophet is accepted in the prophet's hometown. 25 But the truth is, there were many widows in Israel in the time of Elijah, when the heaven was shut up three years and six months, and there was a severe famine over all the land; 26 yet Elijah was sent to none of them except to a widow at Zarephath in Sidon. 27 There were also many lepers in Israel in the time of the prophet Elisha, and none of them was cleansed except Naaman the Syrian." 28 When they heard this, all in the synagogue were filled with rage. 29 They got up, drove him out of the town, and led him to the brow of the hill on which their town was built, so that they might

hurl him off the cliff. [30] But he passed through the midst of them and went on his way.

First Response (4:22)

Jesus had read Isaiah 61:1–2a, which taught that God's Messiah would be good news to all kinds of marginalized people, such as "the poor," "the captives," "the blind," and "the oppressed" (Luke 4:18). He then claimed the words of Isaiah found fulfillment in him. In my opinion, Jesus here staked a claim to be the Messiah. Jesus used Isaiah's words to define the thrust of his ministry.

Try to imagine the various ways people in the crowd might have processed Jesus' words. Most no doubt knew of his growing fame as a teacher and healer. Some probably thought he might well be a prophet. Now he spoke as if he thought himself to be the promised Messiah. One thing is certain: most in the crowd knew him as the son of Joseph. They had watched Jesus grow from childhood to young adulthood. Many knew him as a carpenter. They also knew him as a fellow member of their synagogue.

Luke records their initial response to Jesus as somewhat ambiguous yet positive. On the whole, they thought well of Jesus. Perhaps they also liked how his growing fame reflected on their town. Wouldn't it be wonderful if Nazareth might soon claim to have produced a prophet? Some, though, no doubt wondered how the man they knew could possibly be a prophet, let alone the Messiah.

As for the possibility Jesus might be the Messiah, perhaps they hoped it proved true—after a certain fashion. When they heard the words of Isaiah, they thought of themselves. When the Messiah came, he would come to them and set them free of Roman oppression. While the Messiah would be good news to people like themselves, they believed he would be bad news to the Romans and to Gentiles in general. If Jesus should prove to be that kind of Messiah, they would support him.

Jesus Pushed the Envelope (4:23–27)

Jesus sensed the crowd's hopes. He refused to adjust his mission to fit their theological package. Rather than play to their desires, he called them to accept a larger vision of God's grace. Jesus used a variety of means to do so.

First, Jesus brought some of their deepest concerns to light. For example, I think the phrase "doctor, heal yourself" is best interpreted to mean *doctor, heal your own people first*. If Jesus was the great healer/physician, why had he not already done miracles in Nazareth, his hometown? Such an interpretation fits well with the statement that follows: "Do here also in your hometown the things that we have heard you did at Capernaum" (Luke 4:23).

Jesus tried to help the people see their tendency to restrict the scope of God's ministry. Using some imagination, we might paraphrase part of his message to them as follows:

> I see into your hearts, and I know many of you think I should have started my ministry here in Nazareth. You want to hear me teach with power, as I've done in Capernaum. You want to see me do other things as well, perhaps give actual sight to the blind and do other similar things. Most of all, I think, you want me to establish my base here in Nazareth. You want the fame that would come your way. You want the Messiah to belong only to you.

Second, Jesus cited a common proverb: "No prophet is accepted in the prophet's hometown" (4:24). We understand the proverb's obvious meaning: family and friends find it hard to accept that we might take on a role beyond that which they've known. Jesus also used the proverb to set the stage for a startling proposition: God's redemptive work included the Gentiles as well as the Jews.

Jesus drew on two familiar stories from the Hebrew Bible to make the point. The story of Elijah and the widow at Zarephath in Sidon is found in 1 Kings 17:8–24. Second Kings 5:1–14 tells about Elisha and Naaman.

While all Israel suffered from a drought and famine, God's prophet Elijah found refuge with a Gentile widow. God worked two miracles on behalf of the widow. First, God multiplied the small amount of grain and oil she had, so that the prophet, the widow, and her only son had food enough. Second, when the widow's son died from a sudden illness, God used Elijah to raise him from the dead. All these things happened while God continued to use the drought and famine to punish the people of Israel for their idolatry.

Naaman the Gentile served a Gentile king. When Naaman contracted leprosy, a Hebrew slave girl directed him to Elisha. At first the proud man refused to go. Even after he relented and visited the prophet, he balked at doing what Elisha told him to do, namely wash in the Jordan River. Another servant persuaded him to try. When he bathed in the river, his leprosy was healed. God healed the Gentile Naaman, even though many lepers among the people of Israel at the time remained unhealed.

Jesus made his point. Through Elijah and Elisha, God dealt not only with his chosen people but with the Gentiles. In fact, in periods when God's people lived under judgment because of their sins, God ministered to a poor Gentile woman, to her son, and to a mighty Gentile warrior. Since God's ministry through such prophets included the Gentiles, how much more must God's Messiah be both for Jew and Gentile? Jesus' ministry would be for all people.

God Cannot Be Stopped (4:28–30)

The synagogue crowd turned angry and dangerous. They forced Jesus from the synagogue and herded him toward a cliff. The crowd intended to throw Jesus off the cliff, probably to disable him in preparation for stoning. In any case, Jesus confounded them. Luke records that Jesus "passed through the midst of them and went on his way" (Luke 4:30). We do not know how he did this, but the story strongly implies the crowd could not lay hands on him. At the very least, Luke intends us to realize the crowd could not hinder Jesus' mission. With or without their support, Jesus set out to be God's good news to all kinds of people.

The Lesson in Life

A Christian man I know became burdened for young men addicted to powerful drugs. He especially wanted to help those to whom the courts had given a last option: stay clean of drugs or go to prison for a long time. My friend founded a nonprofit to provide housing and an in-house counselor for such people.

He asked his church to provide space for the group's weekly meeting. Some wondered whether the church's ministry should include drug addicts. With some nervousness, the church cooperated. As a result, dozens of young men found faith in Christ and a new life beyond the drug culture. After a few years, the ministry took on a life of its own. To this day, its "graduates" continue to help others escape the grip of drug addiction and experience the love of God in Christ.

My friend and his church embraced Jesus' mandate to minister to all kinds of people. Have you made the same commitment?

ELIJAH AND ELISHA

Elijah lived in Israel in the ninth century B.C. He especially opposed Queen Jezebel and her efforts to foster idolatry in Israel. Elijah's best known adventure was his confrontation with the priests of Baal at Mount Carmel (1 Kings 18:20–38). He also announced the coming of a multi-year drought as a manifestation of God's judgment (1 Kings 17:1). During the time of the drought, Elijah took refuge in Sidon, a Gentile territory. While Elijah usually worked alone, he took on at least one disciple: Elisha. When Elijah was carried off to heaven, Elisha succeeded him.

Elisha's ministry followed Elijah's. At God's command, Elijah anointed him as his successor (1 Kings 19:19–21). He ministered for approximately fifty years.

People in the time of Jesus held both prophets in high esteem. Elijah and Elisha were held in the kind of esteem we reserve for George Washington and Abraham Lincoln. Jesus used the stories of these popular prophets to insist God's mission included not only the Jews but the Gentiles.

APPLYING THE LESSON

- Pray and ask God to help you identify ways in which you resist the scope of his mission

- Make a list of people groups you think your church might have trouble believing God intends to touch with his love in Christ

- Take the list and do an online search for stories about people or churches who have developed ministries to such groups

- Invite the leader of a local nonprofit devoted to ministry to a challenging people group to speak to your class about the challenges and opportunities of such ministry

QUESTIONS

1. Reflecting on the story of the church and the people in the trailer park, how do you think your church family might have responded?

2. Have you ever experienced a time when a wise church leader helped the church see a ministry opportunity it had overlooked?

3. Why do you think the synagogue worshipers became so angry when Jesus cited the Elijah and Elisha stories?

4. Do you think God excludes any people group from his concern and love? If not, why do we sometimes do so?

LESSON TEN

*Called to Gather People
for the Kingdom*

MAIN IDEA

In response to God's grace, we are to join Jesus on his mission and gather people for his kingdom.

QUESTION TO EXPLORE

How does your life match up with Jesus' call to gather people for his kingdom?

STUDY AIM

To identify ways I will respond to Jesus' call to gather people for Jesus' kingdom

QUICK READ

Jesus called his first disciples to work with him to gather people into his kingdom. In spite of their fears, they did so.

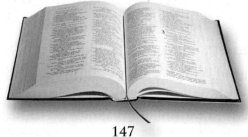

Work consumed most of my grandmother's waking hours on the family farm. She got up early to prepare breakfast, helped milk thirty cows, prepared lunch, milked the cows a second time, and cooked dinner as well. At night she might help one of us with homework or work on the farm's account books.

My grandmother worked hard, but what she liked most was to fish. Whenever she could carve some time from her workday, she dug some worms, loaded the cane fishing poles in the back of the truck, and headed for a nearby small lake. Most of the time, she took me along. She wanted to teach me how to fish.

Naturally, this took some work the first time I went fishing with her. My grandmother cast her line smoothly, dropping the bait and float just where she aimed. I swung my pole wildly and managed to snag my line high in the trees behind us. She favored me with a sad look and then patiently stretched to reach into the tree. The line hung fast. She tugged harder and harder. Finally, the line released, and the float flew out and hit her square in the head.

She shook her head and then quietly checked to make sure my hook was still baited. She took the pole from me and said, "Now watch. I'll show you how to do it." A moment later the hook and float settled lightly onto the lake water. Then she said, "Now, pull your line out gently and try again." She could tell I was afraid, and so she added, "Don't worry. I'm here. I'll help you get the hang of it." And she did.

I started to become a fisherman that day. You might say my grandmother *called* me to join her in the sport.

LUKE 5:1–11

[1] Once while Jesus was standing beside the lake of Gennesaret, and the crowd was pressing in on him to hear the word of God, [2] he saw two boats there at the shore of the lake; the fishermen had gone out of them and were washing their nets. [3] He got into one of the boats, the one belonging to Simon, and asked him to put out a little way from the shore. Then he sat down and taught the crowds from the boat. [4] When he had finished speaking, he said to Simon, "Put out into the deep water and let down your nets for a catch." [5] Simon answered, "Master, we have worked all night long but have caught nothing. Yet if you say so, I will let down the nets." [6] When they had done this, they caught so many fish that their nets were beginning to break. [7] So they signaled their partners in the other boat to come and help them. And they came and filled both boats, so that they began to sink. [8] But when Simon Peter saw it, he fell down at Jesus' knees, saying, "Go away from me, Lord, for I am a sinful man!" [9] For he and all who were with him were amazed at the catch of fish that they had taken; [10] and so also were James and John, sons of Zebedee, who were partners with Simon. Then Jesus said to Simon, "Do not be afraid; from now on you will be catching people."

[11] When they had brought their boats to shore, they left everything and followed him.

Down by the Lake (5:1–3)

Jesus returned to Galilee after a brief excursion into Judea. He once again began to teach by the lakeside. The Gospel of Luke identifies the lake in an unusual way: "the lake of Gennesaret." "Gennesaret" was the name of the Gentile territory on the other side of the lake from Galilee. By using the term, the Gospel of Luke gently reminds us Jesus' ministry touched both the Jews and the Gentiles. We most often call the lake the *Sea of Galilee.*

The Sea of Galilee is large, about thirteen miles in length from north to south and about eight miles across at its broadest. In places, the depth may reach 200 feet. A fishing industry thrived along its shores. Fishermen used a variety of nets, but when boats were in play they most often deployed what is called a trammel net. The boats formed a circle and then closed toward one another to trap fish in the nets.

Fishermen usually fished at night. Fish rose from the depths during the night, making it easier to catch them. The realities of the fish market also drove the fishermen's schedule. They had to prepare the night's catch for the market. Afterwards they dried and repaired their nets in preparation for another night's fishing.

Jesus' arrival interrupted the business day. Imagine the busiest shopping mall in your city. Now picture Jesus arriving along with a large crowd, stepping onto a food court table, and teaching. While many people might flood the mall to see and hear him, none of them would be shopping. Would-be customers who had come to the mall to shop would probably be annoyed. Delivery people could not get in or out of the mall easily. All the normal routines would grind to a halt or at least slow to a crawl. Your own employees would become distracted. If you were a business owner, how might you feel?

A Miraculous Catch (5:4–7)

Jesus knew one of the fishermen, Simon. Earlier he had healed Simon's mother from a deadly fever (Luke 4:38–39). Perhaps this explains why Simon quickly agreed to put his boat back in the water so Jesus might teach from it.

We do not know how long Jesus taught. Simon kept the boat in place the entire time. Doing so threw Simon's typical day off schedule, but he willingly made the sacrifice.

Simon probably thought his task had ended when Jesus finished teaching. Much to his surprise, Jesus told him to take the boat out into the deep water and let down his nets. Simon already respected Jesus as a miracle worker and a teacher, but he could tell Jesus was no fisherman. No one who knew anything about serious fishing would fish during the day. Besides, Simon's crew was exhausted after having fished all night without success.

Still Simon obeyed. He and his crew rowed to deep water and let down their nets. Almost immediately the nets filled with fish to the point of breaking. Simon called out for help from his partners. Even with additional boats, the catch proved challenging. The boats began to sink.

All the fishermen, including James and John, were amazed. Simon, though, fell to his knees before Jesus. As would often be the case in the future, Simon got out a little ahead of the others. He said to Jesus, "Go away from me, Lord, for I am sinful man" (Luke 5:8). The term "Lord" signaled something important. At least in that moment, Simon saw God present in Jesus in a special way. Simon knew he stood in the presence of the Holy. Like Isaiah (Isaiah 6), he responded by confessing his sinfulness and admitting his unworthiness.

While we cannot know the tone of Simon's statement, I think sadness colored it. Unable to imagine God could want or use a person like him, Simon saw no option but to ask Jesus to go away.

That being said, I can imagine an alternative interpretation. Simon was a successful small business owner. He employed a crew of fishermen, owned a house in the city, and enjoyed his place in the community. Simon's life was well ordered. Perhaps he feared a "Lord" who might shake up his long-established world view and routine.

Other interpretations may occur to you. In any case, Simon asked Jesus to leave. He never dreamed Jesus might have other plans in mind.

Come Learn to Fish (5:8–11)

Jesus said, "Do not be afraid" (5:10). The angel used a similar phrase with Mary (1:30), when he told her she would bear "the Son of the Most High" (1:32). Luke wanted his readers to realize Simon was now caught up in the larger story God was writing: the story of the Messiah. Jesus saw the fear of personal unworthiness or change that lay behind Simon's words and acted to calm it.

Simon must have been startled by what followed. Jesus said, " . . . from now on you will be catching people" (5:10). Kneeling there in the boat, surrounded by the miraculous catch of fish, Simon could not miss Jesus' point. Jesus wanted Simon to join him in the work of gathering people into the kingdom of God. Simon, who had spent his lifetime learning how to catch fish, would now learn how to draw men and women to Jesus.

We might say Jesus offered Simon a job. The other Gospels tell how Jesus called the first disciples to come and follow him. Luke's Gospel stresses a different emphasis: the life-defining task Jesus gave them. Keep in mind our previous study of Luke 4:14–21. "Catching people" involved reaching out to all kinds of people, sharing the good news of redemption, and working toward social justice.

Simon and the others brought their boats to shore. Simon, James, and John then "left everything and followed him" (5:11). The phrase is subject to various interpretations. For example, it might mean they immediately followed him, leaving behind their wet nets, boats, and fish. That's remarkable enough in itself. Seasoned fishermen followed a routine designed to protect their investment in boats and nets and maximize their sales in the fish market. They broke from good business practice to follow Jesus. Other fishermen must have thought them unhinged.

They probably left the tasks to their employees and family members. We know the business remained intact, for some of them evidently returned to it for a time after the death of Jesus (see John 21). Still, as all small business owners know, it's risky to leave your company in anyone else's hands. No one takes care of the company quite like the owner. Leaving their affairs in the hands of others entailed a significant risk.

Here's the thing to note: *they took action.* They actually walked away from their established way of life, followed Jesus, and tried to learn how to gather people for the kingdom of God. Contrast this with our tendency to read Scripture, debate its meaning in a Bible study group or with friends, and then return to our normal lives. We too often are like the Sunday class that spent an hour studying the Bible's teachings on feeding the hungry and then adjourned for lunch at a local restaurant. The story of the call of Simon challenges us to step out of routines and help others see, acknowledge, and enter the kingdom of God.

The Lesson in Life

Real people today join Jesus to gather people for his kingdom.

A friend of mine works two part-time jobs, but he lives to draw people to Jesus. When he noticed a local motel had become home to many low-paid workers and their families, he investigated. He discovered that many of the families lacked access to healthy food, necessary clothing, and medical care. Most had no connection to a church.

My friend attends a small church that some would describe as *blue-collar*. He shared his concern with his church. After prayer and reflection, the church decided to try to be God's good news to the people living at the motel. They started a monthly program. As my friend put it, "We decided to throw a party for all those people." Each month the church provides a festive meal. They also offer clothing and other necessary items. Good music sets the mood. As the ministry has grown, the church has found ways to provide medical screening, tutoring, and other services. They also provide opportunities for Bible study and worship.

I often talk with my friend about the motel ministry. In his typical, colorful fashion he once said to me: "We're learning how to fish with Jesus. You have to go to the people."

FISHING IN THE SEA OF GALILEE

The Sea of Galilee was also called the Lake of Gennesaret and the Lake of Tiberias in the time of Jesus. Towns and villages surrounded the fresh-water lake. Capernaum was one of the major towns near the lake and a center of the fishing industry.

Fish provided most of the meat protein consumed in the area. Fishermen sold their fresh catch in nearby marketplaces. Fish were also salted, pickled, or dried for shipment to Jerusalem and other locations. Fishermen fished from shore and in boats.

Fishermen depended on the lake for their livelihood, but they did not trust its weather. Afternoon storms frequently swept down from the surrounding highlands. The weather often settled during the evening and night hours.

APPLYING THE LESSON

Try the following exercises to help you apply the lesson:

- Take a Sunday afternoon and drive around your town looking for places where you or your class might develop a ministry

- Consider linking with another church who already has a ministry to an under-reached group of people

- Try to make a list of actions your class might take this week or month to introduce specific people or people groups to the love of Christ

- Pray and ask God to fill you with the desire to partner with Jesus to gather people for his kingdom

QUESTIONS

1. Have you ever broken from your daily or business routine in order to help Jesus gather people for his kingdom? Do you know someone who has done so?

2. Using your imagination, how do you think others
   might have reacted when Simon, James, and John
   "left everything" to go with Jesus (Luke 5:11)?

3. Have you ever felt an urge to try to introduce others
   to Jesus through your words and deeds?

4. Reflecting on the lesson, what would it take to convince you to make changes in your life so that you might help Jesus gather people for his kingdom?

LESSON ELEVEN
Jesus' Life-Altering Instructions

MAIN IDEA

Disciples are to live Jesus' life-altering instructions, even though they go against the grain of our culture.

QUESTION TO EXPLORE

Why do we generally spend more effort explaining away Jesus' instructions than living them?

STUDY AIM

To decide how I will respond to Jesus' instructions

QUICK READ

Jesus calls us to embrace his kind of life and live it. We often have to lay aside culturally-conditioned attitudes and ways in order to do so.

Over lunch one day, some friends and I discussed following Jesus. One of them made a comment that got my attention. He said, "Do you realize American Christianity is the first Christianity in history to ask what's the least we have to do to go to heaven?" He got it right, didn't he? Most of the time that's how we approach following Jesus.

Such an approach robs us of the challenge and joy of growing in the likeness of Christ. Jesus, of course, had much more in mind for his followers. He envisioned us learning to trust God enough to turn loose of cultural norms and live as he lived. The more we do so, the more we find ourselves thinking and living in ways that go against the grain of our culture. Jesus knew we needed instructions, and he provided them in what many call his "Sermon on the Plain."

LUKE 6:17–46

17 He came down with them and stood on a level place, with a great crowd of his disciples and a great multitude of people from all Judea, Jerusalem, and the coast of Tyre and Sidon. **18** They had come to hear him and to be healed of their diseases; and those who were troubled with unclean spirits were cured. **19** And all in the crowd were trying to touch him, for power came out from him and healed all of them.

20 Then he looked up at his disciples and said:

"Blessed are you who are poor,

for yours is the kingdom of God.

21 "Blessed are you who are hungry now,

for you will be filled.

"Blessed are you who weep now,

for you will laugh.

22 "Blessed are you when people hate you, and when they exclude you, revile you, and defame you on account of the Son of Man. **23** Rejoice in that day and leap for joy, for surely your reward is great in heaven; for that is what their ancestors did to the prophets.

24 "But woe to you who are rich,

for you have received your consolation.

25 "Woe to you who are full now,

for you will be hungry.

"Woe to you who are laughing now,

for you will mourn and weep.

26 "Woe to you when all speak well of you, for that is what their ancestors did to the false prophets.

27 "But I say to you that listen, Love your enemies, do good to those who hate you, **28** bless those who curse you, pray for those who abuse you. **29** If anyone strikes you on the cheek, offer the other also; and from anyone who takes away your coat do not withhold even your shirt. **30** Give to everyone who begs from you; and if anyone takes away your goods, do not ask for them again. **31** Do to others as you would have them do to you.

32 "If you love those who love you, what credit is that to you? For even sinners love those who love them. **33** If you do good to those who do good to you, what credit is that to you? For even sinners do the same. **34** If you lend to those from whom you hope to receive, what credit is that to you? Even sinners lend to sinners, to receive as much again. **35** But love your enemies, do good, and lend, expecting nothing in return. Your reward will be great, and you will be children of the Most High; for he is kind to the ungrateful and the wicked. **36** Be merciful, just as your Father is merciful.

37 "Do not judge, and you will not be judged; do not condemn, and you will not be condemned. Forgive, and you will be forgiven; **38** give, and it will be given to you. A good measure, pressed down, shaken together, running over, will be put into your lap; for the measure you give will be the measure you get back."

39 He also told them a parable: "Can a blind person guide a blind person? Will not both fall into a pit? **40** A disciple is not above the teacher, but everyone who is fully qualified will be like the teacher. **41** Why do you see the speck in your neighbor's eye, but do not notice the log in your own eye? **42** Or how can you say to your neighbor, 'Friend, let me take out the speck in your eye,' when you yourself do not see the log in your own eye? You hypocrite, first take the log out of your own eye, and then you will see clearly to take the speck out of your neighbor's eye.

43 "No good tree bears bad fruit, nor again does a bad tree bear good fruit; **44** for each tree is known by its own fruit. Figs are not gathered from thorns, nor are grapes picked from a bramble bush. **45** The good person out of the good treasure of the heart produces good, and the evil person out of evil treasure produces evil; for it is out of the abundance of the heart that the mouth speaks.

46 "Why do you call me 'Lord, Lord,' and do not do what I tell you?

Down From the Mountain (6:17–19)

Jesus retreated to a mountain to pray overnight. Such retreats may have helped Jesus clarify his vision and discern his next steps. His first followers slowly learned from Jesus' example. Early in the history of the church Christians began to try to build such retreats into their lives, whether through daily prayer times or more formal retreats. We live busy lives. My hunch is many of us take little time to slow down, reflect on the teachings of Jesus, and pray. If Jesus found such retreats necessary, we certainly need them as well.

When morning arrived, Jesus came down from the mountain to level ground. There he found a large crowd of people waiting for him. They came from various cities and towns. Most likely all were Jewish, but the list of cities and towns suggests that some Gentiles may have been present as well. Perhaps Jesus' vision of God touching both Jew and Gentile had already begun to be realized.

Jesus chose to turn his attention from the large crowd to a much smaller group. He selected twelve of his followers to be his apostles. While Jesus continued to minister to crowds and other individuals, he now focused most of his attention on the apostles. He set out to teach them how to live his kind of life, how to take on his outlook and ministry.

Blessings and Woes (6:20–26)

"If you don't want your world turned upside down, stay away from Jesus," a friend of mine used to say. Jesus did not set out to confirm his apostles' culturally-conditioned assumptions and practices. Instead he gave them instructions for living that ran counter to their normal aspirations. He couched his instructions in the form of blessings and woes.

The term often translated "blessed" might also be rendered as *happy* or *truly happy*. People of God in the first century, like most of us today, sought happiness. They held firm ideas about what made for happiness: marriage, children, good health, business success, living to a ripe old age, and the like. To their credit, many also thought worship, prayer, and helping the poor mattered. Still, in practice most people structured their lives around comfort.

Try to catalog your personal criteria for happiness. To put it another way, what makes you feel blessed? A good friend who is not a Christian tells me he feels blessed when he has some money tucked away, plenty to eat, reasonably good health, and no one out to get him. I've thought a great deal about his perspective. It's old. You can find similar hopes expressed in some ancient Greek philosophies, portions of the Hebrew Bible, and advice columns in modern newspapers or on line.

Jesus took a radically different approach. He told his disciples they might be blessed by poverty, hunger, grief, and persecution. If you're like me, you're more familiar with Matthew's version of the Beatitudes (see Matthew 5:2–12). Matthew focused on spiritual yearnings. Luke, though, gave Jesus' words a more nearly literal interpretation. We must take Luke's understanding of Jesus seriously. Certainly the first-century crowd did. They understood the term "poor" to refer to day laborers, widows, orphans, and all those who eked out a living. Hunger accompanied such poverty, as did grief. When Jesus said "poor," very specific images from real life filled the minds of his hearers.

Jesus' disciples lived in a world where most believed poverty and misfortune to be signs of God's judgment. Many of us may harbor a similar belief. Most believed wealth to be proof of God's blessing. In fact, they often spoke well of the wealthy and disparaged the poor. How many of us tend to follow a similar pattern?

Jesus took the opposite view. He insisted the experiences in Luke 6:20–23 might prepare a person to live the kind of life Jesus lived. Jesus went against the grain of his culture, and he called his disciples to do the same.

Intentional Love Is the Key (6:24–36)

The worn maxim says: "Don't get mad, get even." Jesus' listeners understood the sentiment. For the most part, they approved it. Jesus taught and modeled the opposite approach. He advocated the practice of intentional love toward all, even enemies.

Jesus' examples invoked strong feelings from his listeners. They lived under the rule of Rome. Many knew directly, or through others, how it felt to be misused or cursed by a Roman soldier. Tax collectors employed by Rome regularly defrauded Jesus' listeners. They dreamed of revenge. Many assumed God's Messiah would lead a successful revolt against Rome. They could not imagine God might want them to treat their oppressors well.

Yet Jesus called them to do so. He noted people of all cultures tend to love those who treat them well. He insisted his followers must go further. Loving one's enemies marked one's growing maturity in Christ and prepared one to live as a citizen of God's kingdom.

As time went by, many would-be Jesus followers deserted him over this issue. His closest disciples struggled to learn the way of love toward all. Choosing to embrace a way of life that runs contrary to our culture is hard!

Do Not Judge (6:37–42)

Jesus continued to drive home the contrast between culture's assumptions and his own. He lived in a culture of written and unwritten rules. People tended to pass judgment on one another and on entire classes of people. We might almost say passing judgment was not only assumed to be right but a duty. Jesus took the opposite approach and called his disciples to follow his lead.

By means of two parables, Jesus gently ridiculed the practice of passing judgment. The first pictured a blind person trying to lead another blind person only to guide them both into a pit. The second featured a man with a log stuck in his eye trying to remove a splinter from another person's eye. Such parables were a little like political cartoons today: they used humor to make a telling point. In this case, Jesus tried to teach his disciples that their own sin rendered them incapable of accurately judging others.

Jesus told them God's kingdom functioned on the basis of forgiveness and mercy. If they wanted to become the kind of people who would be at home in God's kingdom, they must learn to practice such virtues. When I reflect on the teaching, I often ask myself: *Am I becoming the kind of person who would enjoy living in God's kingdom, or would I be startled and confused by the dominance of grace and forgiveness I found there?*

Shaped by Obedience (6:43–46)

Jesus told his disciples to look at their deeds to determine how well they followed him. He compared our lives to a fruit tree. Each kind of tree is known by its particular fruit. Jesus insisted his followers would produce actions and attitudes similar to his own.

Note the realism of Jesus. He acknowledged his own disciples might call him Lord yet not do what he told them to do. As you read through Luke's Gospel, you will see how often the apostles failed. If we take a few moments to think, we find the same is true of ourselves. Why do we find it so hard to accept and practice the teachings of Jesus? Two answers come to mind: the power of personal sin and the power of sin ingrained in culture.

Such sin pushes us to look for exceptions or to explain away Jesus' instructions. In my birth culture we often sought to limit the scope of Jesus' commands. For example, one of our favorite sayings was: "I'll turn the other cheek, but if you hit that cheek, I'm free to strike back." Have you ever said something similar?

One of my Sunday School teachers believed firmly in the limits of forgiveness. He had fought in World War II. In his heart, he could not believe God expected him to forgive either the Germans or the Japanese. Whenever he taught today's Scripture passage, he stumbled badly as he tried to explain away the clear meaning of Jesus' words.

LESSON 11: *Jesus' Life-Altering Instructions*   171

Most of us tend to resist Jesus whenever his teachings challenge our experience or culture.

Jesus calls his disciples to follow him. Following Jesus changes us. Such changes inevitably challenge many of our personal and cultural assumptions. The more readily we turn loose of the old and take hold of the new, the more we become people in whom others can see Jesus.

The Lesson in Life

Once a month or so, I eat lunch with a man who is not a Christian. We've forged a friendship over the past few years. I enjoy our conversations. My friend is well read and thoughtful. In fact, he probably knows the Bible better than most Christians. He loves Jesus, but he is not impressed by Christians.

"I don't think you Christians take Jesus seriously," he often says. "I mean, if you did, would I hear so many Christians on radio calling for revenge against their enemies? Don't get me started on the crusades! To be honest, it seems to me that Christians like to be associated with Jesus but don't want anything to do with his way of life."

Such conversations might take a different direction if more of us chose to follow the life-altering instructions of Jesus.

BEATITUDES

Jesus did not invent the literary form called *beatitudes*. Instead he learned the form from the Hebrew Scriptures, the Old Testament as we call it.

Most Old Testament beatitudes occur in the Psalms, the worship book of Israel. Examples can be found in Psalms 1; 2; 41; 65; 84; 106; 112; and 128. Proverbs 8:32; Isaiah 32:20; and Daniel 12:12 provide additional examples. Those who heard Jesus use the form were as familiar with it as we are with hymns and choruses.

Beatitudes usually begin with an assertion: *Blessed is* or *Happy is*. The assertion is followed by a brief description of the kind of person who is so blessed. For example, Psalm 1:1–2 declares: "Happy are those who do not follow the advice of the wicked, or take the path that sinners tread, or sit in the seat of scoffers; but their delight is in the law of the LORD, and on his law they mediate day and night."

APPLYING THE LESSON

- Think about how non-Christians see Christians. Do non-Christians tend to see Christians negatively or positively? Why?

- Take a piece of paper and write one or two paragraphs on how your life reflects Jesus' life-altering instructions.

- Take a piece of paper and write one or two paragraphs on how you resist Jesus' life-changing instructions.

QUESTIONS

1. Reflecting on the lesson, how do you respond to the statement: "Do you realize American Christianity is the first Christianity to ask what's the least we can do to go to heaven?"

2. Have you ever known someone who chose not to take seriously the instructions of Jesus as found in today's Scripture lesson? If so, why do you think he or she did so?

3. What do "enemies" deserve from Christian men and women?

4. What reasons do we give for resisting the life-altering instructions of Jesus?

LESSON TWELVE

Where Forgiveness Leads

MAIN IDEA

The greatness of our love for God and other people is related directly to our recognition of the greatness of God's forgiveness of our sins.

QUESTION TO EXPLORE

To what extent do your actions toward God and other people indicate recognition of how far God had to go to forgive you?

STUDY AIM

To analyze how I have responded to God's offer of forgiveness

QUICK READ

Jesus taught we love God and others in proportion to how much we sense our common need for God's forgiveness.

That fellow does not belong with decent folk. Have you ever heard someone say something along those lines? Likely you have. We've probably encountered such sentiments even in church.

Bobby comes to mind. We went to school and church together. Bobby came from a poor family. They lived at the edge of town in a substandard house. His father worked occasionally at odd jobs, but he spent most of his time intoxicated. All the children in the family had to fend for themselves. By the time Bobby started school, he knew how to lie, bully, cheat, and steal. He probably needed such skills to survive his home life.

Looking back, I see we did not treat Bobby kindly. We children feared him, and we soon learned how to keep him at the edge of our games and groups. Even adults tried to hold Bobby at a distance. In addition to fear, I now realize we looked down on Bobby. Frankly, we thought ourselves righteous, especially in comparison to Bobby and his family.

To our surprise, Bobby came to our little church one Sunday morning. He stood just inside the door looking confused. None of us knew what to do. I shall never forget the woman who got up, went to him, and took him to sit next to her. Throughout the service, she helped him find the Scripture readings and hymns. She stayed with him at the end of the service, and she introduced Bobby to the pastor and others.

Something good started that day, not only for Bobby but for the rest of us as well. With her help, he began to break free from the life he had known. She also pushed the pastor and the rest of us to take an interest in Bobby. After a while, our perspective changed. We started to treat Bobby as if he were part of our group. Some years later, he became a Christian.

Years later the woman who befriended Bobby told some of us about her motivation. She said, "Most of you don't know this, but in my early life my family made some mistakes. I did, too. I did not know about the love of God or how to serve God. Later, though, with the help of some people I changed. I turned my life over to God. I felt the forgiveness of God. I still do. When I looked at Bobby I saw someone like me, and I knew I had to try and help him."

Her experience of forgiveness pushed her to love God and others. Perhaps she knew the story of Jesus, the Pharisee, and the woman as told in Luke 7:36–50.

LUKE 7:36–50

36 One of the Pharisees asked Jesus to eat with him, and he went into the Pharisee's house and took his place at the table. **37** And a woman in the city, who was a sinner, having learned that he was eating in the Pharisee's house, brought an alabaster jar of ointment. **38** She stood behind him at his feet, weeping, and began to bathe his feet with her tears and to dry them with her hair. Then she continued kissing his feet and anointing them with the ointment. **39** Now when the Pharisee who had invited him saw it, he said to himself, "If this man were a prophet, he would have known who and what kind of woman this is who is touching him—that she is a sinner." **40** Jesus spoke up and said to him, "Simon, I have something to say to you." "Teacher," he replied, "speak." **41** "A certain creditor had two debtors; one owed five hundred denarii, and the other fifty. **42** When they could not pay, he canceled the debts for both of them. Now which of them will love him more?" **43** Simon answered, "I suppose the one for whom he canceled the greater debt." And Jesus said to him, "You have judged rightly." **44** Then turning toward the woman, he said to Simon, "Do you see this woman? I entered your house; you gave me no water for my feet, but she has bathed my feet with her tears and dried them with her hair. **45** You gave me no kiss, but from the time I came in she has not stopped kissing my feet. **46** You did not anoint my head with oil, but she has anointed my feet with ointment. **47** Therefore, I tell you, her sins, which were many, have been forgiven; hence she has shown great love. But the one to whom little is forgiven, loves little." **48** Then he said to her, "Your sins are forgiven." **49** But those who were at the table with him began to say among themselves, "Who is this who even forgives sins?" **50** And he said to the woman, "Your faith has saved you; go in peace."

Dinner at a Pharisee's House (7:36–39)

Jesus confounded expectations as he ministered in Galilee. He healed the slave of a Gentile centurion and pronounced the centurion's faith superior to any he had found in all Israel (Luke 7:1–10). Jesus felt compassion for a widow whose only son had died. Jesus raised him from the dead, thus providing for the woman's economic well-being (7:11–17). His actions confused the Pharisees, other religious leaders, and even John the Baptist. Jesus did not meet their expectations (7:18–35).

Some chose to test Jesus. A Pharisee named Simon invited Jesus to dinner at his house. Dinner guests normally removed their sandals. A good host greeted his invited guests with a kiss, water with which to wash their feet, and the like. When ready, the dinner group reclined on low couches. In the house of a Pharisee, dinner conversation might well deal with the religious law. Simon probably anticipated using the occasion to probe Jesus' teachings and behavior. The Pharisee hoped to label Jesus as righteous or unrighteous.

Such dinners sometimes attracted outsiders. Even people considered sinners might gather around the dining group to listen to their conversation. No one took any notice of them. The uninvited guests were supposed to remain silent and not interact with the dinner party.

A woman known to belong to the class of "sinner" arrived. The Scriptures do not tell us the nature of her sin. She may have been unable to afford to keep the purity laws. Perhaps she had a disease that rendered her ritually unclean. Most commentators assume she practiced prostitution. A single woman without a family might well be forced by financial need to become a prostitute.

Whatever the woman's particular transgression might have been, Simon regarded her as a sinner. As one of the righteous, he avoided direct contact with her, lest he be contaminated by her sin.

The woman broke the rules. She wept, kissed the feet of Jesus, anointed them with ointment, and dried them with her hair. From our vantage point, the woman's actions may appear pious. The Pharisee, though, lived in a different time. He thought the woman's behavior outrageous. A known sinner had no standing before the righteous. She should have remained silent, kept her distance, and been content to be tolerated. Simon felt well within his rights to evict her, perhaps even to arrange for some kind of punishment.

The Insight of Jesus (7:39–43)

Jesus' quiet acceptance of the woman and her actions offended Simon. In his view, a genuine prophet would have known the woman to be a sinner and recoiled from contact. Simon believed Jesus should have rejected the woman's actions and condemned her.

Simon never imagined he and the woman shared a common problem called sin. Jesus discerned Simon's thoughts and moved to correct him. Note that Simon called Jesus "Teacher" (7:40). Given Simon's frame of mind, he probably used the term sarcastically. Jesus ignored the implied insult, told a parable, and posed a question.

The parable spoke of two people in debt to the same person. One owed fifty denarii , the other five hundred denarii. A denarius was roughly equal to what a modern person might earn in one day at minimum wage. In all likelihood, both debtors were day laborers. The two debtors shared a common condition: poverty. Neither one had any realistic hope of paying the debt.

Simon and the others around his table did not know how the parable would end. They probably anticipated punishment for both debtors. Jesus surprised them when he said the creditor forgave both debts. I suspect Simon found the parable puzzling. What did debtors have to do with him? He thought he owed nothing to anyone, including God.

Jesus tried to open Simon's mind. He asked Simon which debtor would love the creditor more. Simon answered he supposed the one forgiven of the greatest debt. Jesus told him he had given the correct answer.

A Telling Comparison (7:44–46)

Looking at the woman, Jesus compared Simon to her. No one anticipated Jesus' doing so. Simon and most other people did not believe such a comparison possible. In Simon's worldview, he and the woman had nothing in common. She was a sinner, and he was a righteous man. Jesus denied the distinction. He insisted Simon and the woman lived with the same debilitating condition: sin. Both were sinners in need of God's forgiveness.

Simon revealed his shortcomings by how he treated Jesus. Even though he invited Jesus to dinner, he treated Jesus as an inferior. Contrary to custom, Simon did not provide water to cleanse Jesus' feet or oil with which to anoint his head. He did not greet Jesus with a kiss. In short, Simon believed himself in a position to pass judgment on Jesus. He condescended to give Jesus an opportunity to prove Jesus belonged in Simon's company!

The woman, whom Simon judged beneath his notice, practiced every courtesy toward Jesus. She anointed Jesus' feet, dried them, and even kissed them. Her tears revealed her humility. She sought God's forgiveness. The woman did not put Jesus to a test. She came to him as a debtor, daring to believe he might cancel her debt.

Jesus' words must have startled everyone present, including Simon and the woman. He reversed the normal order of things. Jesus approved the woman and her actions and found Simon wanting.

Judgments (7:47–50)

Jesus announced God's judgment of the woman and declared her many sins forgiven. He praised her for relying on God's mercy rather than her own righteousness. Jesus suggested the woman would love God more because she felt the greatness of God's forgiveness.

Jesus also passed judgment on the mindset of Simon, and those who shared it. He implied they could not love God or others well until they surrendered their ingrained self-righteousness.

The table guests tried to judge Jesus. How dare he claim to be able to forgive sins? Surely only God could do so. Luke's account captures the irony of their statements. Yes, only God could forgive sins. They, the religious leaders, could not see God was present at the table in the person of Jesus. Only the "sinner" woman saw with clear sight.

The Lesson in Life

If you go to lunch at a certain pizza parlor in Memphis, Tennessee, you may encounter a man I'll call Jeff. Jeff is an ordained minister who makes his living as a sales representative. As Jeff puts it, the pizza parlor is his church field. Many years ago, he decided to try to reach the artists and students who live in the area. Many of them eat at the pizza parlor several times a week.

Jeff loves to tell how the experience changed him.

When I started, I told myself I was going to where the sinners could be found. I hate to admit it, but I thought of myself as a righteous person out to rescue the unrighteous. I felt awfully proud of myself. The people could sense my attitude, and they kept their distance. One day while I sat eating pizza, a thought popped into my head. "I'm just like a stereotypical Pharisee!"

Anyway, the moment I realized I was nothing more than a sinner eating among sinners, something started to happen. The folk in the pizza parlor started to accept me. We began to get to know one another. I learned about their jobs and families, their fears, and even their hopes. They paid attention when I talked about my life and faith. Some even became Christians.

Here's the thing. I learned to love them, and some of them came to love me. It's strange, but the more I recognized our common need, the more free I became to trust God and simply love them.

FORMAL DINNERS

We find it difficult to imagine the setting for a formal dinner such as the one Jesus attended at Simon the Pharisee's house. The dinner may have been held inside a house or in a courtyard. Either way, custom allowed uninvited guests to stand at a respectful distance and listen to the conversation.

Guests reclined on low couches or pillows. The food was served on a low table or mat, and the guests leaned on one arm and ate with the other. Their feet faced away from the table.

Think of such dinners as public forums, in which guests expected to discuss important matters. The crowd listened carefully, both for entertainment and to learn. Subjects varied with the nature of the hosts. If the dinner took place in the home of a notable Gentile, the guests might discuss literature, politics, or similar matters. Pharisees devoted themselves to learning, interpreting, and applying the religious laws. Their dinner discussion usually focused on some disputed point of the law.

APPLYING THE LESSON

- Pray and ask God to help you see your sinfulness and seek his forgiveness

- Use your imagination and ask: If I had been at Simon's dinner, what might I have thought of the woman?

- Take a piece of paper and make a list of all the ways you know you fall short of God's intentions for you.

Pray and ask God to remind you of your need for his forgiveness as you deal with other people each day.

- Try to identify two or three people whom you tend to regard as undesirables or sinners.

- Pray that God will teach you to respect and love them as fellow sinners in need of God's grace.

QUESTIONS

1. As you read the story of Bobby, what came to mind?

2. Why do you think the Pharisee invited Jesus to dinner?

3. Why do you think Jesus accepted the dinner invitation?

4. What element in the Scripture passage most challenges you? most challenges your church?

Journeying to Jerusalem

The four lessons in this unit are from the section unique to the Gospel of Luke that tells of Jesus' journey to Jerusalem and the cross. Large crowds followed Jesus seeking healing and instructions. The religious leaders became increasingly hostile to Jesus and looked for ways to trap him. Outcasts were attracted to Jesus' compassion and power.

Throughout these chapters Jesus rebuked the religious leaders and encouraged the marginalized. Jesus used parables to teach the principles of the kingdom of God and characterized the kingdom as a celebration. Even though Jesus was drawing nearer to the cross, he reached out mercifully to the crowds and wanted to gather them to himself.

The church must listen carefully to Jesus' instruction to the religious leaders. Too often we are like the older brother left in the fields, rather than partners with the Father welcoming home the prodigal. We often are critical of the lost, and we neglect the very ones Jesus came to save. Jesus calls out to the church and invites us to join him in welcoming the poor, the sick, and the sinful to the messianic celebration.[1]

UNIT FOUR: JOURNEYING TO JERUSALEM

NOTES

1. Unless otherwise indicated, all Scripture translations in unit 4, lessons 13—16, are from the New American Standard Bible (1995 edition).

LESSON THIRTEEN

A Narrow Door, a Limited Time

MAIN IDEA

God's gracious offer of salvation requires a specific response and is available only for a limited time.

QUESTION TO EXPLORE

How wise is it to live as if life has no limits and we are fully in control?

STUDY AIM

To recognize the urgency of a right response in light of the demands attached to God's offer of salvation

QUICK READ

Where do we stand with God? Salvation is neither universal nor automatic. In Luke 13:3, 5, Jesus tells us to repent or perish. In Luke 13:22–35 we are reminded that the door to eternal life is narrow and the time to respond is limited.

Someone asked Jesus, "Lord, are there just a few who are being saved?" (Luke 13:23). Jesus didn't respond to the question directly but asked rather whether the person himself was ready.

This is the question of the ages and the topic Jesus discussed as he moved toward Jerusalem. Thousands of folks were following him (see 14:25). Jesus was healing the sick and teaching insights about the kingdom through parables. Religious leaders were stalking Jesus and trying to discredit him. But Jesus was not distracted by the threats of his opponents or the praise of the multitudes.

What did the person mean when he asked about salvation? Jesus answered by speaking of the kingdom of God. He explained that a day of separation was coming when some would enter a place of torment while others would dine at the table with the saints from throughout the ages. The text in this section of the Gospel of Luke refers to the recognition of limits—a narrow door (13:24), a limited time (13:25), a response required (13:25b–30), Jesus' destiny in Jerusalem (13:31–34), and tragedy ahead (13:35).

We first must respond to Jesus' teaching individually. *What is my relationship with Christ?* Then we should ask ourselves how we are to communicate this urgency to our family, friends, and neighbors and even to strangers. All who were listening to Jesus were religious. All were children of Abraham. Most lived strict, morally upright lives. Yet not all would enter through the narrow door. Jesus clearly warned in Luke 13:3, 5 that either we repent or we perish. "If anyone wishes to come after Me, he must deny himself, and take up his cross daily and follow Me" (9:23).

LUKE 13:22–35

22 And He was passing through from one city and village to another, teaching, and proceeding on His way to Jerusalem. **23** And someone said to Him, "Lord, are there just a few who are being saved?" And He said to them, **24** "Strive to enter through the narrow door; for many, I tell you, will seek to enter and will not be able. **25** "Once the head of the house gets up and shuts the door, and you begin to stand outside and knock on the door, saying, 'Lord, open up to us!' then He will answer and say to you, 'I do not know where you are from.' **26** "Then you will begin to say, 'We ate and drank in Your presence, and You taught in our streets'; **27** and He will say, 'I tell you, I do not know where you are from; depart from Me, all you evildoers.' **28** "In that place there will be weeping and gnashing of teeth when you see Abraham and Isaac and Jacob and all the prophets in the kingdom of God, but yourselves being thrown out. **29** "And they will come from east and west and from north and south, and will recline at the table in the kingdom of God. **30** "And behold, some are last who will be first and some are first who will be last." **31** Just at that time some Pharisees approached, saying to Him, "Go away, leave here, for Herod wants to kill You." **32** And He said to them, "Go and tell that fox, 'Behold, I cast out demons and perform cures today and tomorrow, and the third day I reach My goal.' **33** "Nevertheless I must journey on today and tomorrow and the next day; for it cannot be that a prophet would perish outside of Jerusalem. **34** "O Jerusalem, Jerusalem, the city that kills the prophets and stones those sent to her! How often I wanted to gather your children together, just as a hen gathers her brood under her wings, and you would not have it! **35** "Behold, your house is left to you desolate; and I say to you, you will not see Me until the time comes when you say, 'Blessed is He who comes in the name of the Lord!'"

The Question of the Ages (13:22–30)

Every religion deals with the question of what happens after this life. Most offer hope for those who fulfill the sacred obligations set out by their religion. Atheists believe there is no life after this one, and agnostics claim there is no way one can know. The vast majority of Americans believe in God and that they are going to heaven. If there is a hell, many think the notoriously wicked will be the only ones who go there.

Our society appears to support and propagate the notion of salvation by death. We often hear that those who have died have gone to a better place regardless of the kind of life they may have lived. Perhaps the church's lack of urgency in evangelism indicates that even the church has bought into this notion.

Jesus clearly taught that salvation is not guaranteed to all. He referred in these verses to the inevitable Day of Judgment and the fact that some will be saved and others will not. "And someone said to Him, 'Lord, are there just a few who are being saved?'" (13:23). Jesus responded, "Strive to enter through the narrow door; for many, I tell you, will seek to enter and will not be able" (13:24). Salvation requires a response from the one who wants to receive it.

In the Sermon on the Mount, Jesus said, "Enter through the narrow gate; for the gate is wide and the way is broad that leads to destruction, and there are many who enter through it. For the gate is small and the way is narrow that leads to life, and there are few who find it" (Matt. 7:13–14).

In Luke 13:6–9, Jesus told the parable of a fig tree that bore no fruit. In the parable, the man who had the fig tree told the "vineyard-keeper" to cut it down. The "vineyard-keeper" requested more time but agreed that after that the unproductive fig tree should be cut down. The parable reminds us there will be a final chance to respond and the time is limited.

In Luke 13:25, once the head of the house closed the door, it would be too late for those still on the outside. The ones who were excluded from the banquet were surprised.

They claimed to have known the Lord and even to have had fellowship with him. But Jesus will say, "'I tell you, I do not know where you are from; DEPART FROM ME, ALL YOU EVILDOERS'" (13:27).

In Genesis 6, God announced to Noah the coming destruction of the world. Noah faithfully preached God's message to his contemporaries while he worked on the ark (see also 1 Peter 3:20; 2 Peter 2:5). Yet when Noah and his family entered the ark and God closed the door, it was too late for those who had failed to believe. Jesus said, "For the coming of the Son of Man will be just like the days of Noah. For as in those days before the flood they were eating and drinking, marrying and giving in marriage, until the day that Noah entered the ark, and they did not understand until the flood came and took them all away; so will the coming of the Son of Man be" (Matt. 24:37–41).

The New Testament consistently defines the Day of Judgment as a time of separation of the righteous and the unrighteous. The ones who seek to establish their own righteousness will fall short, and only those who stand in the righteousness of Christ will be saved. Our deeds reflect our heart.

The synagogue leader in Luke 13:10–16 was more interested in the interpretation of the Sabbath than in the needs of a woman who had been sick for eighteen years. He missed a relationship with God and settled for religious activity.

People from all over the world will be present at the table in the kingdom of God. There will be many surprises in our eyes. Jesus says the last will be first and the first last. One would have expected the synagogue leader to have been favored by God, and yet Jesus gave attention instead to the woman who was ill. Samaritans, Galileans, prostitutes, and tax collectors were often closer to the kingdom than the religious.

The Son of God was standing in their presence. His deity had been attested by signs and miracles. Yet the religious leaders and many of the crowd were so preoccupied by their own beliefs and priorities that they failed to heed Jesus' message.

The temptation to follow our own path persists today. We let the daily routines and challenges of our lives take precedence over the urging of the Spirit and the pleading of Scripture. Some crowd out the longing to know God with busy lives and selfish agendas. Others substitute religious activities and rituals for a personal vibrant relationship with God. Yet others who come before God with brokenness and humility and throw themselves onto God's mercy will find themselves dining at the messianic table in the kingdom of God.

A Price to Be Paid (13:31–35)

God's gift of grace comes with a price. Jesus continued heading to Jerusalem for his appointment with the cross. Nothing would deter him.

Some Pharisees approached Jesus and warned him that Herod wanted to kill him (13:31). We cannot know whether their motives were based on a genuine interest in Jesus' welfare or they were simply attempting to get him out of their community. Jesus wasn't afraid of or impressed by Herod; in fact, he called him a "fox" (13:32). Some believe this reference indicates that Herod was sly or crafty; others, that he was destructive. Yet rabbinical writings at the time used the metaphor of a fox to describe one who was insignificant. How could the King of kings be frightened by the king of Galilee?

Jesus declared that he "must" journey on to Jerusalem. The verb "must" is a strong word (13:33). God's plan was already set. Jesus would go to Jerusalem and there offer his life as a ransom for our sins. The city chosen as the host site for God's temple would become known as the city that killed the prophets.

Jesus would soon reach his goal, Jerusalem (see 13:33). Perhaps Jesus was in southern Perea, still under Herod's jurisdiction, and two days' journey to Jerusalem. The expression "today and tomorrow and the next day" may have had an additional significance, indicating also that on the third day Jesus would be raised from the dead.

Jesus' statement in verse 34 indicates he had often wanted to gather Jerusalem under his wing as a hen protects her brood. Jesus must have fervently prayed for the city. How could a city that had witnessed so many of the blessings and evidences of a gracious God been so blind to God's Son when he came?

When Jesus walked through the streets of Jerusalem, he saw the sick, the poor, and the oppressed. The temple had become a place of commerce instead of a house of prayer. Religious leaders were often false prophets protecting their own positions, twisting God's word, and turning rich symbols and rituals of God's grace into systems of oppression and exploitation. Jesus loved Jerusalem and longed to save her.

What does Jesus see when he looks at our cities today? Voices of victims who are oppressed are still crying out. Mistreatment of the poor and the strangers continues. Pleasure has become a god. People live with indifference to eternity and desire religions that condone their vices.

What does God hear coming from our churches? Does God hear cries of repentance and brokenness and voices of praise and adoration? Does God hear prayers of intercession for the lost and see acts of kindness when God's people reach out even to those who ridicule them? Too often God finds pride and arrogance and hears petty theological arguments while lost neighborhoods are neglected and people perish without hearing the hope of Christ. Luke 13 reminds us that the door to eternal life is narrow and the time is limited.

The Lesson in Life

We must first ask God to examine our own hearts. *What is my relationship with Christ? Is there evidence in my life that God has done a transformational work? Am I more concerned about my own religious standing than I am about the needs of those who surround me? Am I becoming more like Christ? Or am I becoming judgmental and hardened?* Come before God with humility and repentance, and ask for God's grace and mercy.

We need to allow God to impress on us our responsibility to share the good news of Christ with those who do not know him. Who are the members of our family who give no indication of walking with Christ? Who are our neighbors or work associates who are unchurched? Does your church have the urgency for the lost that Jesus demonstrated in this passage?

HEROD

Several Herods are mentioned in the New Testament. Below is a list of who they were. Herod the tetrarch is the one mentioned in Luke 13.

1. Herod the Great (born about 73 B.C.) was king of the Jews 40–4 B.C. Although he rebuilt the Jewish temple in Jerusalem, he never endeared himself to the Jewish people. Herod was a violent king who

was suspicious of any potential rival, including his own sons. Matthew 3 records Herod's slaughter of the young boys in Bethlehem.

2. Archelaus ("Herod the Ethnarch" on his coins) reigned in Judea "in place of his father Herod" (Matt. 2:22) from 4 B.C. to A.D. 6, but without the title of king.

3. Herod the tetrarch (see Luke 3:19) bore the distinctive name of Antipas. He inherited Galilee and Perea from his father. He was the one who imprisoned and executed John the Baptist and was called "that fox" by Jesus in Luke 13:32.

4. "Herod the king" (Acts 12:1) was otherwise known as Agrippa (reigned A.D. 41–44). He sought the good will of the Jewish people and probably attacked the apostles in Acts 12 because of their relationship with Gentiles. His sudden death is recorded by Luke in Acts 12.

5. Agrippa II, son of Herod Agrippa, was born in A.D. 27. When the Apostle Paul stood before Agrippa telling him his faith story, Agrippa asked whether Paul was attempting to make him a Christian (Acts 26:28).

APPLYING THE LESSON

- Who is someone in your circle of influence who gives no evidence of knowing Christ?

- How can you pray for him or her?

- How can you get to know this person's story? What are his or her interests, passions, and needs?

- What steps need to be taken to win the person's trust?

- How can you tell this person about the difference Christ makes in your life?

QUESTIONS

1. How did Jesus respond to the question in Luke 13:23, "Lord, are there just a few who are being saved?" What do you think he meant?

2. What did Jesus mean when he said the first will be last and the last first (13:30)?

3. What ethnic groups from non-Christian cultures live in your community? How can you build bridges of trust with them?

4. How can we take the hope of Christ to the people around the world who have never heard the message of Christ?

LESSON FOURTEEN

Priority Matters

MAIN IDEA

What God values takes precedence over religious rituals, human ambition, and the agendas of ordinary life.

QUESTION TO EXPLORE

What truly takes priority in our lives?

STUDY AIM

To identify ways Jesus' teachings call for a reordering of my priorities

QUICK READ

Jesus compared the kingdom of God with a banquet. Two questions arise from these parables: will you be present? will you bring anyone with you?

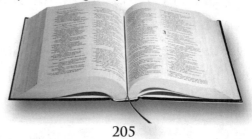

Is it really true that everyone loves a party? We have all been to grueling events that are anything but fun. I have attended wedding dinners that were exciting and entertaining, but not nearly all of them fit that description. After officiating hundreds of weddings and eating tons of white cake, I wouldn't describe these events as some of my fondest. Then, of course, there are the formal dinners where you *must* attend, wear uncomfortable clothes, and carry on meaningless conversations with strangers.

However, the idea of a banquet is a fascinating way to describe the kingdom of God. I think of it more as a Hebrew festival where folks gathered with friends and family for food and fellowship, perhaps like a family reunion.

When I was a child, our family would gather at my grandparents' house with my cousins, aunts, and uncles. Everyone brought good Southern cooking. For two or three days we laughed, ate, played, and told stories. These were events we didn't want to miss.

In Luke 14:15 one of the guests said, "Blessed is everyone who will eat bread in the kingdom of God." He was right, although he might have been presumptuous. It may never have entered his mind that he might not be one of those present. After all, he was a descendant of Abraham and a religious man.

Jesus never questioned the idea of the messianic banquet. Jesus did explain, though, that some would miss out because of misplaced values. For some people, religious rituals, human ambitions, and busy lives would take precedence over God's invitation to join Jesus in kingdom living.

LUKE 14:1–24

[1] It happened that when He went into the house of one of the leaders of the Pharisees on the Sabbath to eat bread, they were watching Him closely. [2] And there in front of Him was a man suffering from dropsy. [3] And Jesus answered and spoke to the lawyers and Pharisees, saying, "Is it lawful to heal on the Sabbath, or not?" [4] But they kept silent. And He took hold of him and healed him, and sent him away. [5] And He said to them, "Which one of you will have a son or an ox fall into a well, and will not immediately pull him out on a Sabbath day?" [6] And they could make no reply to this. [7] And He began speaking a parable to the invited guests when He noticed how they had been picking out the places of honor at the table, saying to them, [8] "When you are invited by someone to a wedding feast, do not take the place of honor, for someone more distinguished than you may have been invited by him, [9] and he who invited you both will come and say to you, 'Give your place to this man,' and then in disgrace you proceed to occupy the last place. [10] "But when you are invited, go and recline at the last place, so that when the one who has invited you comes, he may say to you, 'Friend, move up higher'; then you will

have honor in the sight of all who are at the table with you.
[11] "For everyone who exalts himself will be humbled, and he who humbles himself will be exalted." [12] And He also went on to say to the one who had invited Him, "When you give a luncheon or a dinner, do not invite your friends or your brothers or your relatives or rich neighbors, otherwise they may also invite you in return and that will be your repayment. [13] "But when you give a reception, invite the poor, the crippled, the lame, the blind, [14] and you will be blessed, since they do not have the means to repay you; for you will be repaid at the resurrection of the righteous."
[15] When one of those who were reclining at the table with Him heard this, he said to Him, "Blessed is everyone who will eat bread in the kingdom of God!" [16] But He said to him, "A man was giving a big dinner, and he invited many; [17] and at the dinner hour he sent his slave to say to those who had been invited, 'Come; for everything is ready now.' [18] "But they all alike began to make excuses. The first one said to him, 'I have bought a piece of land and I need to go out and look at it; please consider me excused.' [19] "Another one said, 'I have bought five yoke of oxen, and I am going to try them out; please consider me excused.' [20] "Another one said, 'I have married a wife, and for that reason I cannot come.' [21] "And the slave came back and reported this to his master. Then the head of the household became angry and said to his slave, 'Go out at once into the streets and lanes of the city and bring in here the poor and crippled and blind and lame.' [22] "And

the slave said, 'Master, what you commanded has been done, and still there is room.' ²³ "And the master said to the slave, 'Go out into the highways and along the hedges, and compel [them] to come in, so that my house may be filled. ²⁴ 'For I tell you, none of those men who were invited shall taste of my dinner.'"

Don't Be Misled by Religious Rituals (14:1–6)

Jesus was invited to a religious leader's home on the Sabbath for dinner. It was likely a setup. The Pharisees and scribes had become hostile to Jesus and were plotting against him (Luke 11:53). A man was present who had a disease called "dropsy" (14:2). That is, his limbs were swollen with excess body fluids. The Pharisees and experts in the law watched to see whether Jesus would heal the man on the Sabbath.

God had created the Sabbath for people as a time of rest and worship. However, religious leaders perverted it with rituals and laws that made it a burden. A meal could not even be cooked on the Sabbath. The bread set before the guests at the meal would have been prepared earlier. Even the rules for keeping the food fresh and for warming it were highly regulated. Jesus claimed to be from God. Surely *Jesus* knew it was forbidden to heal on this day. How could Jesus be authentically from God if he violated the Sabbath?

These professors of the law had spent their lives learning, discussing, and teaching God's commandments. They lived highly moral lives and never missed religious practices. Yet they apparently had little concern for one of God's children standing before them hurting, and they didn't even recognize the Messiah.

Jesus asked, "Is it lawful to heal on the Sabbath, or not?" (14:3). According to the law of Moses, work was prohibited on the Sabbath, but *work* was not actually defined. Law experts drafted dozens of declarations about what was work and what wasn't. The Gospels tell of a number of other incidents in which Jesus healed on the Sabbath (see Matthew 12:9–14; Mark 3:1–6; Luke 6:6–11; 13:10–17; John 5:1–18; 9:1–41). Jesus used these opportunities to teach the valuable lesson that people are more important than religious rituals. When Jesus asked whether healing on the Sabbath was lawful, the Pharisees remained silent.

Jesus reached out to the man, healed him, and sent him away. He then asked the poignant question, "Which one of you will have a son or an ox fall into a well, and will not immediately pull him out on a Sabbath day?" (Luke 14:5). (The King James Version has "ass or an ox" instead of "son or an ox." Most scholars agree that the older and preferred reading is "son.") How perverted for religious leaders to be more concerned about a religious ruling made by human beings than about a person created in the image of God who was standing before them. They were unable to answer Jesus' question.

It is easy for Christians to say we *hate the sin but love the sinner.* Yet how many people we consider notorious sinners are actually welcome in our services? Is it possible that we too have become so bogged down in our traditions and rituals that the unchurched feel unwelcome in our midst? A woman who was faced with serious addictions was asked whether she had tried church. She answered, "Why would I go there? I feel guilty enough as it is."

Don't Be Blinded by Human Ambitions (14:7–15)

Jesus noticed that the guests at this dinner were trying to sit in places of honor at the table. He said, in effect, *Don't sit at places of honor at an event. Someone more important may show up, and then you will be asked to move to a lesser position. If you sit in an humble place, and your host invites you to move to a prominent place, then you will receive honor among the guests* (14:8–10).

Jesus was not playing to people's ambitions by sharing a shrewd plan for personal exaltation. Rather he was teaching the biblical principle that the first will be last and the last first. The setting was the home of "one of the leaders of the Pharisees" (14:1). Power and prestige are often huge temptations for leaders. In the case of the Pharisees, much of their opposition to Jesus came from his threat to their authority. Their motives were often exposed by Jesus' actions and teachings.

Even the followers of Jesus had to fight the desire for status and special treatment. In Matthew 20:20–28, the mother of the sons of Zebedee asked Jesus to allow her boys to sit at Jesus' right and left in the kingdom. The other ten disciples became indignant when they learned of her request.

At a banquet in that day, the seats of privilege were those nearest the honored guest at a dinner. Today, in military formal events, seating is arranged by rank. Even two people of the same rank are positioned based on the one who achieved the rank first. James wrote of a situation in the early church in which the rich were given places of favoritism in the assembly, and the poor, wearing dirty clothes, were pushed aside (James 2:1–7). James asked, "Listen, my beloved brethren: did not God choose the poor of this world to be rich in faith and heirs of the kingdom which He promised to those who love Him?" (James 2:5).

Jesus told his host not to invite those who could repay him, such as friends, relatives, or the rich. "But when you give a reception, invite the poor, the crippled, the lame, the blind, and you will be blessed, since they do not have the means to repay you; for you will be repaid at the resurrection of the righteous" (Luke 14:13–14).

Don't Be Distracted by Busy Lives (14:16–24)

The invitation to the dinner went out first to guests who were considered prominent. Each, though, gave an excuse for not attending. Their lives were too busy with vocations and relationships for them to consider the opportunity to be important.

Romans ate four times a day. Greeks ate three times a day. Hebrews ate twice, once in the morning around 10 o'clock and another time around sunset. Obviously, the banquet would not have been in the morning, and so it had to be a dinner. Invitations were sent out twice—once, several days in advance, and the second time on the day of the event once preparations were complete. Because of this, the guests had plenty of time to plan ahead.

However, the first person gave the excuse that he had bought some land and needed to go and see it. It is highly unlikely he would be seeing his land at night and *after* buying it rather than before. The second person bragged that he had bought five yoke of oxen. Since the average Palestinian was fortunate to have one or two oxen, this excuse was like saying, *I can't come because I have to test drive my new luxury car.* The third excuse was more understandable. This guest said, "I have married a wife" (Luke 14:20). (One can read into that excuse whatever he or she wishes!) Obviously, even though the invited guests must have initially accepted the invitation, the banquet was not a priority for any of them. Their lives were full enough without including another activity.

The head of the household heard the report from his slave and was angry. He said, "Go out at once into the streets and lanes of the city and bring in here the poor and crippled and blind and lame" (14:21). Yet even some of them may have refused the invitation because there was still room. Then the master said, "Go out into the highways and along the hedges, and compel them to come in, so that my house may be filled. For I tell you, none of those men who were invited shall taste of my dinner" (14:23–24).

Jesus' implication must have been obvious to the host, who was a leader of the Pharisees. Twice Jesus mentioned the outcasts. If the prominent refuse the invitation to the banquet, bring in the marginalized; if they refuse, invite the heathen.

The tax collectors and the sinners of this time were more open to the gospel than the religious leaders were. Ultimately, even many of them would reject the gospel, and the invitation would be extended to the Gentiles.

My wife and I once had an opportunity to attend the Brooklyn Tabernacle Church in New York City for a Tuesday night prayer meeting and Sunday morning worship. We had dinner with some of the staff before the prayer meeting, and they said they would reserve seats for us. I had never been in a church that needed crowd control for a prayer meeting. It was shocking to see the 1,500-seat auditorium with standing room only. As we observed those attending and heard some of their stories, we realized that many of them had once been outcasts. Jesus' forgiveness really was good news for them.

One of the reasons many churches are empty is we have run out of people like us to invite. We fail to realize that the ones most open to Christ have always been those who were hurting and seeking or those who have never heard. Many whose lives are filled with vocations, wealth, friends, and even religion fail to value the privilege of coming to the kingdom dinner. The Master, who has paid a great price for the banquet, rejects our flimsy excuses for not attending; he lovingly calls the lost to join him.

Jesus' first invitation to us is to join him for the Messianic meal. He then invites us to go out in his name and welcome others to attend. How will we share this summons with the poor, the sick, and the neglected? How will we get this good news to those who have never even heard? The time of the dinner is at hand, and the invitation is urgent.

Implications for Today

The good news of Luke 14 is that the kingdom of God is a Messianic banquet. The bad news is that many whose lives are so full and whose priorities are so foolish will miss the banquet. Are we like the religious leaders who focus on the law and miss the Lawgiver? Are we like the people in Jesus' parable who were preoccupied with personal agendas and rejected the invitation?

Does the church carry out the role of the servant whose responsibility is to fill the house with guests for the banquet? Where are the people who are eager and willing to accept the invitation?

THE SABBATH

The Sabbath law is found in various place in the Old Testament (see Exodus 20:8–11; 23:12; 31:12–17; 34:21 35:2–3; Deuteronomy 5:12–15; Leviticus 19:3; 23:3; 26:2). A Bible scholar summarizes, "The Sabbath commandment enjoins absolute rest for all, including servants and animals, on the ground that God made heaven and earth and also redeemed Israel. On the Sabbath (and new moon) business stops, offerings are made, feasts are held, and the man of God may be consulted (2 Kgs. 4:23)."[1]

The rabbis later developed detailed descriptions of what was prohibited. The intent of the further development was to continue to keep a fence around the law but to provide for practical needs as well.[2]

Jesus' relationship to the Sabbath was at the center of much of the conflict with religious leaders. The Sabbath was given as a blessing, but it had become a burden. Jesus said, "The Sabbath was made for man, and not man for the Sabbath. So the Son of Man is Lord even of the Sabbath" (Mark 2:27–28).

APPLYING JESUS' INSTRUCTIONS

Many of the poor in the community today do not have adequate health care. Seek a partnership with health care professionals in your community and sponsor a health fair hosted by the church offering free services in the language of non-English-speaking residents. Create fun activities for the children.

Encourage Christians who speak other languages to reach out to the guests as friends and make audio, video, or language-specific New Testaments available to those who are interested. Build relationships with the health care professionals and the guests, and find opportunities to extend the friendships beyond that day. Have counselors available who will listen to special concerns and who will share the hope of Christ when appropriate.

QUESTIONS

1. What was the religious leader's motivation for inviting Jesus to his house?

2. Who were the poor, the crippled, the lame, and the blind Jesus referred to twice in this passage? Who are they today?

3. How can the servant "compel" those in the highways and hedges to attend?

4. Do any of our religious rituals make it harder for the church to share the love of Christ?

5. Who are the marginalized in our community, and how can we share the good news of Christ with them?

6. Do we have misplaced priorities that blind us to kingdom opportunities?

NOTES —————————————————————————————

1. Gerhard Kittel, Gerhard Friedrich, Geoffrey William Bromiley, *Theological Dictionary of the New Testament* (Grand Rapids, Mich: W.B. Eerdmans, 1995), S:989.

2. *Theological Dictionary of the New Testament*, S:990

FOCAL TEXT
Luke 15:1–2, 8–32

BACKGROUND
Luke 15:1–32

LESSON FIFTEEN

Coming to the Party?

MAIN IDEA

Jesus' life and teachings show that we are to celebrate God's love and grace for *all* people.

QUESTION TO EXPLORE

Are you going to the party celebrating God's love and grace for *all* people?

STUDY AIM

To decide how I will participate in a celebration of God's love and grace for *all* people

QUICK READ

The theme of Luke 15 is the joy that comes from the transformation of the lost. The chapter ends without resolution. Will the older son come to the celebration? Will we?

Is the Christian life a joyful experience for you, or is it a life of duty and rigid obligations? The Pharisees and scribes of Luke 15 appear to have been *painfully* religious. It isn't much of a stretch for us to see the parallel with today's church. We give, attend, and work at the church and in our community often out of guilt and a desire for rewards rather than from an overflow of Christ's joy in our lives. When we read this text, it is sometimes easier to identify with the "righteous" and the older son than with the "sinners" who are redeemed.

Jesus told three stories in Luke 15 in response to the criticism of the religious leaders who accused him of hanging around sinners. As we saw in Luke 14, outcasts and the marginalized came to the kingdom party more quickly than the Pharisees and the scribes. The theme of this chapter is the joy that comes from the transformation of the lost. Perhaps joy is missing from our lives because it has been too long since we have witnessed the rescue and conversion of a person who previously lived without Christ.

Luke 15 ends without resolution. Will the older son come and join the celebration? Will we?

LUKE 15:1–2, 8–32

¹ Now all the tax collectors and the sinners were coming near Him to listen to Him. ² Both the Pharisees and the

scribes began to grumble, saying, "This man receives sinners and eats with them."

• • • • • • • • • • • • • • • • • • • •

8 "Or what woman, if she has ten silver coins and loses one coin, does not light a lamp and sweep the house and search carefully until she finds it? 9 "When she has found it, she calls together her friends and neighbors, saying, 'Rejoice with me, for I have found the coin which I had lost!' 10 "In the same way, I tell you, there is joy in the presence of the angels of God over one sinner who repents." 11 And He said, "A man had two sons. 12 The younger of them said to his father, 'Father, give me the share of the estate that falls to me.' So he divided his wealth between them. 13 "And not many days later, the younger son gathered everything together and went on a journey into a distant country, and there he squandered his estate with loose living. 14 "Now when he had spent everything, a severe famine occurred in that country, and he began to be impoverished. 15 "So he went and hired himself out to one of the citizens of that country, and he sent him into his fields to feed swine. 16 "And he would have gladly filled his stomach with the pods that the swine were eating, and no one was giving anything to him. 17 "But when he came to his senses, he said, 'How many of my father's hired men have more than enough bread, but I am dying here with hunger! 18 'I will get up and go to my father, and will say to him, "Father, I have sinned against heaven, and in your sight; 19 I am no longer worthy

to be called your son; make me as one of your hired men.'"
20 "So he got up and came to his father. But while he was still a long way off, his father saw him and felt compassion for him, and ran and embraced him and kissed him. **21** "And the son said to him, 'Father, I have sinned against heaven and in your sight; I am no longer worthy to be called your son.' **22** "But the father said to his slaves, 'Quickly bring out the best robe and put it on him, and put a ring on his hand and sandals on his feet; **23** and bring the fattened calf, kill it, and let us eat and celebrate; **24** for this son of mine was dead and has come to life again; he was lost and has been found.' And they began to celebrate. **25** "Now his older son was in the field, and when he came and approached the house, he heard music and dancing. **26** "And he summoned one of the servants and began inquiring what these things could be. **27** "And he said to him, 'Your brother has come, and your father has killed the fattened calf because he has received him back safe and sound.' **28** "But he became angry and was not willing to go in; and his father came out and began pleading with him. **29** "But he answered and said to his father, 'Look! For so many years I have been serving you and I have never neglected a command of yours; and yet you have never given me a young goat, so that I might celebrate with my friends; **30** but when this son of yours came, who has devoured your wealth with prostitutes, you killed the fattened calf for him.' **31** "And he said to him, 'Son, you have always been with me, and all that is mine is yours. **32** 'But we had to celebrate and rejoice, for this brother of

yours was dead and has begun to live, and was lost and has been found.' "

The Ministry of Christ (15:1–2)

Jesus was always surrounded by outcasts. The sick, the poor, and the nonreligious flocked to him. Some who came to Jesus lived flagrantly immoral lives. Others followed vocations that were unacceptable to the rigid religious standards of the day. This was proof to the Pharisees and scribes that Jesus could not have been from God. According to them, Jesus was guilty by association.

There were clear distinctions in Jesus' day between the righteous and the sinners. The righteous kept the law, observed the ceremonial cleansings, fasted, prayed three times a day at the temple, and shunned those who did not. The religious avoided the contamination of the irreligious.

The temptation continues for the church today. We brag of our own morality and preach about the transgressions of outsiders. We create our own cloisters and isolate ourselves with Christian activities that keep us away from those who are unlike us. Some Christians honestly don't know anyone personally who is not a Christian.

Jesus was different. Jesus noticed the outsiders. He touched the contaminated. He ate with the immoral. Jesus knew their names. He deplored their destructive habits and would eventually take their sins upon himself. He didn't make them feel comfortable in their sins. Rather he called them to repent. Jesus offered each of them a life of forgiveness, hope, and purpose.

Actually this is why Jesus came. "For the Son of Man has come to save that which was lost" (Matthew 18:11). "So it is not the will of your Father who is in heaven that one of these little ones perish" (18:14).

When Jesus entered Jericho a few chapters further on in this Gospel, he stayed at the house of Zaccheus, a tax collector. The religious leaders were incensed that Jesus chose to single out a sinner rather than one who was righteous. "When they saw it, they all began to grumble, saying, 'He has gone to be the guest of a man who is a sinner'" (Luke 19:7). Yet Zaccheus was transformed. Jesus said, "For the Son of Man has come to seek and to save that which was lost" (19:10).

It makes no sense for a physician to avoid the sick or for the Savior to ignore the lost. When a church fails to connect with the hurting, she misses out on the joy of kingdom living. Jesus illustrated this point with three stories.

The Metaphors of Luke 15

The Lost Sheep (15:3–7). Shepherds were among those considered unclean by the religious because it was impossible for shepherds to keep all of the demands of the interpretations of the law. However, they held a special place in God's plan of redemption. Abraham, Moses, and David were all shepherds. Too, shepherds witnessed the announcement of the birth of Jesus.

A flock of 100 sheep was considered of medium size. Shepherds routinely counted their sheep to ensure none were missing. Because sheep are helpless creatures with no means to defend themselves, a sheep that strayed from the flock was vulnerable to wild beasts, steep cliffs, gorges, and even the harsh Palestinian weather. Shepherds were also in danger when they searched for missing sheep.

A good shepherd knows his sheep and even calls them by name. When a shepherd learns one sheep is missing, he searches for it until he finds it. He scours the rugged terrain, calling out the name of the sheep and praying that he finds it before it is too late. When the shepherd finds the sheep, he puts it on his shoulders and returns to the fold. He probably alternates between expressions of affection for the sheep and stern warnings against future straying.

In the parable, the shepherd later threw a party to celebrate the rescue and called together friends and neighbors to join in the celebration. Jesus said the same thing happens in heaven when one sinner repents.

The Lost Coin (15:8–10). Jesus' second story is about a woman who lost a silver coin, a *drachma*. It may baffle us for someone to be in such a panic over the loss of a coin. However, a drachma represented a day's wages. For families living a day at a time, losing one day's earnings brought immediate hardship.

The significance of the coin might also refer to a head-dress the woman wore, which consisted of ten silver coins that were part of her dowry. To lose a coin from it would be considered an omen of bad fortune.

The woman searched carefully for the coin, but Palestinian houses were usually dark, with no windows and only a small door. The dirt floor was covered with reeds, making the search difficult. In her panic, the woman lit a lantern and swept diligently trying to find the small coin. Perhaps she thought the broom would disturb the straw and a glitter would bring attention to the coin.

The woman was elated when the coin was found. She called together her friends and neighbors to celebrate her restored fortune. Jesus said this is just what the angels in heaven do when one sinner repents.

The Lost Son (15:11–32). Jesus' third parable was about a father who had two sons. The sons were as different from each other as the righteous and sinners who listened to Jesus teach. The older son was dutiful, never neglecting the expectations of being the older son. He also had the most to gain from his father's estate. The oldest son would receive two-thirds of his father's assets, which could be distributed in his father's will or at any time of the father's choosing.

The younger son was impatient. He was tired of the farm and wanted his share now. He believed his life was restricted. He wanted to experience the pleasure and adventure of the far country. His father granted his request.

The younger son went as far as he could from the influences of home and lived without regulations or discipline. While indulging in his heart's desires, he quickly lost everything. Since he was too impetuous to plan, he didn't see the coming famine. He soon found himself without friends, family, or fortune. He was alone in a strange land.

So the son sought work on a farm—probably a lot like the very place he had abandoned. Yet here he was not the owner's son; he was the lowliest of the workers. He was hungry and envied the food the pigs ate. Yet no one gave him anything. At this point, when he realized he had reached bottom, he finally understood what he had forsaken. He knew he would be better off as a day laborer on his father's farm than living in this strange place. It was time to return home and ask for his father's forgiveness.

The father saw the son approaching while he was still far off. The father had obviously been searching the horizon, watching and waiting for the son's return. The father's last prayer in the evenings and his first prayer in the mornings had probably been for his son who was lost. Was he safe? Was he alive?

The father ran to his son, embraced him, and kissed him. The son began to apologize, but the father interrupted with commands to his servants to bring the best robe, a ring, and shoes. This person before him was no slave; he was the father's son.

Farmers customarily kept a fattened calf for special occasions, and this was one of those times. It was time to celebrate because the son who was lost had been found.

The older son who had always followed the rules was so full of bitterness and envy that he shunned the party and scorned his father. Amazingly, the father was just as compassionate to the loveless older son as he had been to the rebellious younger son. The father pleaded with the older son to join the celebration.

The Mission of the Church

The task, values, and passion of the church should be the same as that of Jesus: "to seek and save that which was lost" (Luke 19:10). We must be as courageous as a shepherd, leaving everything behind until we find the one lost sheep; as diligent as a woman looking for a lost coin; and as compassionate as a father welcoming home a rebellious child.

Even though Jesus didn't neglect the religious practices of his day, he also spent much of his time with those who were outcasts. While those who considered themselves pious spent their time debating the Scriptures, observing the rituals, and condemning sinners, Jesus made an effort to comfort the afflicted, heal the sick, and bring hope to the distressed.

How much of the activity and resources of the church are focused on church members? Do we stand at a distance and denounce the sinners? Do we huddle in church buildings and fill our calendars with religious activities to protect ourselves from the contamination of the lost?

Jesus risked criticism and condemnation in his attempt to reach the lost. He had to; that was why he came. His obsession was to bring hope to the hopeless. This is what brought Jesus joy and even brings joy to the angels in heaven. When a church is experiencing the transformation of lives as individuals and families are coming to Christ, the church will enter into the joy of the Lord. When we are not fervent about reaching the unchurched, we are prone to turn inward and become bitter and envious like the older brother.

The Invitation to the Party: Applying the Lesson to Life

God is already working in the lives of those who do not know him, creating conviction and a hunger and restlessness for himself. God has called the church to bring the good news to people.

Jesus has invited the poor, captive, blind, and oppressed (4:18) to the party. The celebration has begun. Will we be a part of it?

DISTINCTION BETWEEN SINNERS AND RIGHTEOUS

In Luke 15:1 "the tax collectors and the sinners" came to Jesus. In verse 2, the religious leaders grumbled about the sinners coming to him. In verses 7 and 10, we find a contrast between the sinners and the righteous. Who were the sinners, and who were the righteous?

In Romans 3:23 we are reminded that we are all sinners. Yet the use of the term in Luke 15 describes a class of people designated sinners by the community. New Testament scholar Joachim Jeremias describes these as people who led immoral lives (such as adulterers and swindlers) and those who followed dishonorable vocations (donkey drivers, tanners, shepherds, peddlers).[1] These people were considered the outcasts of society.

Jesus was probably referring to the religious leaders when he spoke of the righteous. Their dress, activity, behavior, and standing in the community indicated they were righteous. They also were in need of repentance (Matt. 23), but apparently they were unaware of this. In the parable of the Loving Father, the rebellious son was a representation of the sinners and the older son of the righteous. The forgiving love of the Father is there for all of us.

CASE STUDY

Marie has recently moved to the community from another country. She speaks very little English. She is an excellent housekeeper and works for several families from the same church.

Marie is humble and even servile around the families where she works. How can the families build a relationship with Marie? How can they learn her story and her faith background? How can they communicate the love of Christ for her?

QUESTIONS

1. Who were the sinners Jesus referred to in Luke 15?

2. Who were the righteous?

3. Who are the lost in our community?

4. Whom would we classify as sinners?

5. Is our church strategically attempting to reach out to the unchurched with the hope of Christ?

6. Do I know three people who give no indication of knowing Christ for whom I will pray, begin to strengthen the relationship, listen to their story, and look for opportunities to share about Christ?

NOTES ———————————————————

1. Joachim Jeremias, *The Parables of Jesus*, trans. S. H. Hooke, second revised edition (New York: Charles Scribner's Sons, 1972), 132.

FOCAL TEXT
Luke 16:19–31

BACKGROUND
Luke 16:19–31

LESSON SIXTEEN
A Fatal Mistake

MAIN IDEA

How we use our possessions for God's priority of concern for the poor and marginalized of our world shows what our relationship with God really is.

QUESTION TO EXPLORE

What does your use of possessions tell about what you think about God, especially about God's concern for the poor and marginalized of our world?

STUDY AIM

To evaluate how I use my possessions to reflect God's priority of concern for the poor and marginalized of the world

QUICK READ

The consequence of living a selfish life is eternal separation from God. Our response to others in need is an indication of the condition of our heart.

If you want to know the nature of a dog, put a cat in front of it. If you want to know the nature of a Christian, put someone who is hurting in front of him or her. The clearest indication of one who is righteous is sharing the love of God with those who are in need.

Jesus' parables usually begin with an introduction followed by a story, and they conclude with an application. He seldom provided names for the characters. However, this story doesn't follow the same pattern, for in it Jesus used Lazarus's name. Jesus may have been telling a story of two men he knew personally.

The key individual in this story is the unnamed rich man who lived lavishly and wore clothes in his everyday life like the clothes kings wore. He was so preoccupied in his own self-seeking pleasures that he was unaware of the poor man Lazarus who had been dumped at his gate.

When Lazarus died, he was taken by the angels to heaven. When the rich man died, he was plunged into hell.

The purpose of the story is not to say that the wealthy will go to hell. Abraham was also wealthy, and yet he is in heaven. The story reminds us that someone who loves possessions more than the needy among us is a person who does not know God.

LUKE 16:19–31

19 "Now there was a rich man, and he habitually dressed in purple and fine linen, joyously living in splendor every

day. **20** "And a poor man named Lazarus was laid at his gate, covered with sores, **21** and longing to be fed with the crumbs which were falling from the rich man's table; besides, even the dogs were coming and licking his sores. **22** "Now the poor man died and was carried away by the angels to Abraham's bosom; and the rich man also died and was buried. **23** "In Hades he lifted up his eyes, being in torment, and saw Abraham far away and Lazarus in his bosom. **24** "And he cried out and said, 'Father Abraham, have mercy on me, and send Lazarus so that he may dip the tip of his finger in water and cool off my tongue, for I am in agony in this flame.' **25** "But Abraham said, 'Child, remember that during your life you received your good things, and likewise Lazarus bad things; but now he is being comforted here, and you are in agony. **26** 'And besides all this, between us and you there is a great chasm fixed, so that those who wish to come over from here to you will not be able, and that none may cross over from there to us.' **27** "And he said, 'Then I beg you, father, that you send him to my father's house—**28** for I have five brothers—in order that he may warn them, so that they will not also come to this place of torment.' **29** "But Abraham said, 'They have Moses and the Prophets; let them hear them.' **30** "But he said, 'No, father Abraham, but if someone goes to them from the dead, they will repent!' **31** "But he said to him, 'If they do not listen to Moses and the Prophets, they will not be persuaded even if someone rises from the dead.'"

The Contrast Between the Rich Man and Lazarus (16:19–21)

The wealthy appear to be blessed. Their houses, cars, and lavish vacations make it difficult for most other people not to envy them. Of course most folks around the world see average Americans as rich. Some religious leaders today even claim that wealth is a sign of God's favor. Shouldn't children of the King live royally?

Jesus was speaking to the Pharisees, "who loved money" (Luke 16:14). Even though they studied the Scriptures and lived pious and morally upright lives according to the law, many of them still failed to recognize the Messiah when he stood before them. The older son in Luke 15 and the rich man in Luke 16:19–31 were probably references to these Pharisees.

The parable of the rich man and Lazarus paints a horrible picture, describing Jesus' values as opposite of what the religious interpretation of that time would have been. Religious leaders were foolishly comforted by the assumption that God blesses with riches those who fear him and curses with poverty and illness those who do not. Jesus' story probably sounded like blasphemy to the pious.

In the story, Jesus did not give the rich man's name. Perhaps some of the Pharisees who were listening could insert their own names. Can some of us who are reading insert our names?

This man had been deceived by his wealth. He thought his good fortunes were for his own indulgence. He bought lavish clothes and daily dined on banquet foods. He was "joyously living in splendor every day" (16:19).

Wealth promotes a false sense of security. Another prosperous man in Luke 12:19 said to himself, "Soul, you have many goods laid up for many years to come; take your ease, eat, drink and be merry." But "God said to him, 'You fool! This very night your soul is required of you; and now who will own what you have prepared?'" (12:20). When people die, whether they are rich or poor, they leave everything. Wealth provides little security for this life and definitely none for the life to come.

In Luke 16, the rich man's lifestyle of opulence was in direct contrast to Lazarus's poverty. Lazarus had nothing. The Scripture says he was "laid at [the rich man's] gate" (16:20). The word translated "laid" means he was literally *thrown out* at the gate. Lazarus was obviously unable to move himself. He was covered with sores, and he was starving. Dogs were licking his sores. In the story of the prodigal son, the younger son "was longing to fill his stomach with the pods the swine were eating" (15:16, New American Standard Bible, 1977). In the same way, Lazarus longed to eat the crumbs that fell from the rich man's table.

During the time period of this story, napkins or linens were not available for diners to use to clean their hands at the table. Since people ate without utensils, their hands would get soiled. So they would take pieces of bread, dip the bread in a bowl, wipe their hands with the bread, and then throw the scraps under the table. Dogs roaming the room would eagerly eat the scraps or crumbs as they hit the floor. Lazarus was so hungry he craved even the dogs' food.

There is no indication that the rich man abused Lazarus or tried to remove him from the gate. Too, he had obviously learned Lazarus's name. Yet, no sense of inequity, compassion, or urgency compelled him to share with someone whose need was so obvious. The rich man blissfully ate his own food, dressed in his extravagant clothes, and remained unmoved by the plight of another person who, like him, was made in the image and likeness of God but who, unlike him, had nothing.

The Reversal of Fortunes (16:22–26)

Once again, we are reminded that death is no respecter of persons. Both the rich and the poor die.

When Lazarus died, there was no mention of his burial. There would have been no celebration of his life and no public grief for his death for this outcast. But God was always aware of him. Upon Lazarus's death, angels immediately came for him, and they brought him to Abraham's comfort.

Jesus is always aware of the "least of these." In Jericho Jesus stopped to dine with Zaccheus, who was hated as a

Roman collaborator (19:1–10). At the temple, while others watched the influential bring gifts to the treasury, Jesus noticed the poor widow who gave all she had (21:1–4). Jesus touched unclean lepers, dined with notorious sinners, and even called unlearned Galilean fishermen to carry out his mission. It should not be surprising that Lazarus received such a glorious welcome.

The rich man also died and was buried. His family and friends probably celebrated his life. But then he was cast into Hades. There he was in torment. Seeing Abraham and Lazarus at a distance, he begged for relief from his torture. But Abraham told him there was nothing he could do.

This parable is not primarily about heaven and hell, and yet it would be foolish to ignore this description. Very little is said about Lazarus except for the fact that he was escorted by angels and comforted by Abraham. However, the destination of the rich man is frightening. He cried out in pain as he was burned by the flames. Even if Lazarus could dip his finger in water and touch his tongue it would be a relief. Hades is seen as a place of anguish, isolation, and hopelessness.

What was the rich man's sin that brought about this punishment? We usually think of hell as a place for notorious criminals, despots, murderers, and adulterers. There is no indication that the rich man was guilty of anything like this. In fact, he was probably known as a prominent and religious man in his community. All we know about the rich man is that he selfishly indulged himself with his personal possessions and that he neglected Lazarus.

When Jesus described the judgment in Matthew 25, he spoke of a separation of the righteous from the unrighteous. The evidence of righteousness is a person's response to the needy. "Then the King will say to those on His right, 'Come, you who are blessed of My Father, inherit the kingdom prepared for you from the foundation of the world. For I was hungry and you gave Me something to eat; I was thirsty and you gave Me something to drink; I was a stranger, and you invited Me in; naked, and you clothed Me; I was sick, and you visited Me; I was in prison, and you came to Me'" (Matt. 25:34–36).

Does the description in Matthew 25 tell us that acts of kindness will earn salvation for us? No! These expressions of compassion weren't attempts to impress God. The righteous who did these things were not even aware that it was Jesus they were feeding. Acts of love extended to the needy are evidence of a heart transformed by Christ, not actions attempting to merit God's favor. A smoking gun in a murder investigation doesn't make a person guilty; rather it is evidence of guilt. Sharing with those in need, caring for those who are hurting, being friends with those who are rejected—all these things are confirmations that the love of Christ lives within us.

The lack of concern the rich man showed Lazarus was proof of a life of self-centeredness. "But whoever has the world's goods, and sees his brother in need and closes his heart against him, how does the love of God abide in him?" (1 John 3:17). "We love, because He first loved us. If someone says, 'I love God,' and hates his brother, he is a liar; for the one who does not love his brother whom he has seen, cannot love God whom he has not seen. And this commandment we have from Him, that the one who loves God should love his brother also" (1 John 4:19–21).

A Warning to the Living (16:27–31)

When the rich man realized the hopelessness of his situation, he remembered his five brothers. He begged Abraham to send Lazarus to warn them. Abraham reminded him that they had the Scriptures from which to learn. Obviously the rich man had ignored the clear warning of God's word, and he knew his brothers would do the same. Surely if someone came from the dead, it would shock his brothers into belief. But Abraham responded with a difficult statement, "If they do not listen to Moses and the Prophets, they will not be persuaded even if someone rises from the dead" (Luke 16:31).

We are tempted to think the unconvinced will become believers if only they could see something dramatic. Yet when Jesus raised his friend, Lazarus, the brother of Mary and Martha (John 11), some who witnessed the miracle still didn't believe in Jesus, and they plotted to kill him.

In John 6, after Jesus fed the 5,000, the next day the same folks wanted to see another miracle. If God's word did not convince the rich man's brothers, not even a resurrected Lazarus would have changed their lives.

The story of the rich man and Lazarus should awaken us from religious complacency and alert us to the reality of our own lives. Jesus was speaking to some of the most religious people of his day, the Pharisees. They considered themselves children of Abraham. They kept the law. They tithed every leaf in their gardens. They fasted twice a week and prayed three times a day. They studied, memorized, and taught the Scriptures. However, many of them had missed God. Even their religion was about themselves. They were promoters of self and unconcerned about others.

A Personal Application of This Story

How do we know that we know God? Have we convinced ourselves that knowing God comes through religious activity or self-defined morality? Are we counting on church membership, sacred rituals, or even the opinions of others? Have we interpreted our personal successes as blessings from God and proof of God's favor? Are we lovers of money and lovers of pleasure? Are we moved to action by the plight of the poor? Do we share food with those who are hungry?

How do we know our conversion was genuine and our lives have been transformed? The Apostle John wrote, "We know that we have passed out of death into life, because we love the brethren" (1 John 3:14). Our response to the poor and the marginalized is the clearest indication of whether we have been transformed by Christ.

We cannot ignore the urgency of Jesus' teaching. We cannot gamble our eternity on false assumptions or foolish passions. We must not settle for "religion" or worldly pleasures. Such would be a fatal mistake. We must say *no* to our self-centeredness and *yes* to Christ. We must trust Christ to produce his love in us so that we will love others even as he has loved us.

HADES

Hades is the realm of the dead. The Greek word transliterated "Hades" appears ten times in the New Testament—four times in Revelation (Revelation 1:18; 6:8; 20:13; 20:14) and twice each in Matthew (Matt. 11:23; 16:18), Luke (Luke 10:15; 16:23), and Acts (Acts 2:27, 31). In Luke 10:15, Hades is used in contrast to heaven. Peter referred to Psalm 16:10 in the Pentecostal sermon in Acts 2:27, 31, where Hades appears to be a reference to death. Gehenna is usually the fiery place of punishment in the New Testament, but in Luke 16:24 the rich man cried out from Hades to Abraham to send Lazarus to bring relief to him in his agony.

APPLYING THIS SCRIPTURE

- Who are some people in the ministry area of your church who have special needs? Some examples include the hungry; the homeless; the elderly without families; prisoners; children without parents; immigrants who have not become integrated into society; military families in which someone has been deployed.

- Which of these needs best reflects a ministry in which you could participate on a regular basis? How can you build meaningful relationships and give of time and possessions to meet these needs?

- Who are some other people from your church who will minister with you to provide encouragement and accountability?

QUESTIONS

1. To whom was Jesus referring when he spoke of the rich man in this story?

2. Was Jesus teaching that the wealthy cannot go to heaven?

3. What do we learn about heaven and hell in this story?

4. What was the rich man's sin that resulted in his separation from God?

5. What is the basis of your hope for heaven?

6. What actions have I taken in the last month
   that reflect a compassion for the poor and the
   marginalized?

Jesus' Death and Resurrection

Unit five, "Jesus' Death and Resurrection," is a two-lesson study of Luke 23—24. In these chapters, Luke narrates the events of the crucifixion and the resurrection. Earlier in the Gospel of Luke, as Jesus journeyed toward Jerusalem, Jesus knew that the time for his passion had come. The joyful welcome of Jesus by his disciples as he entered Jerusalem (Luke 19:37–38) soon was exchanged for voices shouting for his crucifixion (23:21, 23). Soon as well, a challenge by the Sadducees about the belief in the future resurrection (20:27–38) was followed by Jesus' resurrection as the firstborn from the dead (24:6).

Luke presents us with the question, *Who is Jesus?* The crucifixion and the resurrection reveal who Jesus is. In Luke 22:67, 70, the Jewish religious leaders asked Jesus, "If You are the Christ, tell us. . . . Are You the Son of God then?" Jesus answered and said, "Yes, I am."[1] This confession was the charge against Jesus at his trial, although somewhat politicized (22:71; 23:2). Jesus was crucified based on this charge (23:38). However, Jesus had proclaimed while with the disciples that if he was the Christ he would rise on the third day, and he did (24:46)! Jesus indeed is the Christ. The disciples who witnessed Jesus' resurrection responded with exuberance, for this indeed is good news of great joy (2:10; 24:52).

In our study of Luke 23, Jesus is presented as the innocent Christ. He took the place of Barabbas. Indeed, Jesus takes *your* place. He was mocked, he suffered, and he died on the cross.

The resurrection of Christ is the focus of our study in Luke 24. We are witnesses of that resurrection. Luke shows how the women were the first witnesses of the empty tomb. Other witnesses were the rest of the disciples and the Scriptures.

UNIT FIVE: JESUS' DEATH AND RESURRECTION

NOTES ————————————————————————

1. Unless otherwise indicated, all Scripture quotations in unit 5, lessons 17–18, are from the New American Standard Bible.

FOCAL TEXT
Luke 23:1–26, 32–49

BACKGROUND
Luke 22:14—23:56

LESSON SEVENTEEN
Crucified—for Us

MAIN IDEA

Jesus' crucifixion shows he is truly the Christ of God, God's Chosen One, who provides salvation and is worthy of our full devotion.

QUESTION TO EXPLORE

What makes Jesus' crucifixion so important?

STUDY AIM

To state what Jesus' crucifixion shows about who Jesus is, what Jesus does, and how I am to respond

QUICK READ

Innocent of all charges, Jesus willingly faced the cross as the Chosen One. Taking the place of Barabbas, Jesus died for all the world to see.

The people called me *Barabbas*. On any normal evening one would find me scheming my next plot or heist. However, that evening I sat motionless and gazed into the sunset. People around me were talking about the events of those past few hours. I could not help but stare beyond the walls of the city where the crucifixions had just occurred. Earlier, children had screamed and women wailed when the entire city strangely had been covered in darkness. The ground had shaken, and the Jewish faithful had reported that their temple had been damaged. I recall shivering in the cool evening and rubbing my ankles where the shackles had left my skin open and sore. Yes, I was hurting, but it was nothing compared to the way the teacher had been treated.

The night fell and I could no longer see the sun. I wondered what had happened. I could scarcely take it all in. At the very least, I knew I was not supposed to be alive at that moment. I pinched my arm, wondering whether I was dreaming. The cries of the crowds still echoed in my ears, "Crucify, crucify Him!" (Luke 23:21). I could not believe my ears when the people shouted, "Away with this man, and release for us Barabbas!" (23:18). I still thought it ironic—the crowds did not even know my name. *Bar Abba*, which means *son of the father*, they had called me. To the people,

I was only a pawn in a religious play of power. Yet I knew that I was a despicable rebel, a criminal. The other person—Jesus—the crowd simply called "this man" (23:4). He was not even a political prisoner.

I remember sighing deeply and allowing my thoughts to wander to that awful hill called Calvary. I still wince as I remember how close I came to a horrific death that day. I was the one who had blood on my hands, but that man, whom the crowds called "King of the Jews" (23:3), was perfectly innocent. More than anything, I recall when Pilate brought him out to be released—his eyes met mine. I expected to see hatred and spite. Yet to my amazement, his battered face showed only love. Why this love? Did this man not know that he was facing the cross in my place?

My criminal friends were prepared to throw a party. But, I was in no mood for a celebration. Perhaps someone could explain to this old criminal why my heart was heavy.

In today's text, Luke portrayed Barabbas as the first person for whom Jesus died in his place. We are left to wonder whether Barabbas ever fully grasped what happened that day. Do we fully grasp what happened? What was so important about Jesus' crucifixion? Why is the crucifixion so important to us today?

Jesus' journey toward suffering and death—his passion—began with determination. A definite turning point
occurred in the ministry of Jesus in Luke 9, where Luke
writes, "He [Jesus] set his face to go to Jerusalem" (Luke
9:51; NRSV). From then on, Jesus' teaching focused on his
upcoming suffering and death. Shortly thereafter, Jesus
arrived in Jerusalem with his disciples in time for the
Jewish festival of Passover. As was customary, they had
a Passover meal. Jesus used the occasion of the Passover
meal to institute the Lord's Supper, speaking freely of
his upcoming death. Soon Jesus would be betrayed and
arrested.

LUKE 23:1–26, 32–49

[1] Then the whole body of them got up and brought Him
before Pilate. [2] And they began to accuse Him, saying, "We
found this man misleading our nation and forbidding to
pay taxes to Caesar, and saying that He Himself is Christ, a
King." [3] So Pilate asked Him, saying, "Are You the King of
the Jews?" And He answered him and said, "It is as you say."
[4] Then Pilate said to the chief priests and the crowds, "I find
no guilt in this man." [5] But they kept on insisting, saying,
"He stirs up the people, teaching all over Judea, starting
from Galilee even as far as this place." [6] But when Pilate
heard it, he asked whether the man was a Galilean. [7] And
when he learned that He belonged to Herod's jurisdiction,

he sent Him to Herod, who himself also was in Jerusalem at that time. **8** Now Herod was very glad when he saw Jesus; for he had wanted to see Him for a long time, because he had been hearing about Him and was hoping to see some sign performed by Him. **9** And he questioned Him at some length; but He answered him nothing. **10** And the chief priests and the scribes were standing there, accusing Him vehemently. **11** And Herod with his soldiers, after treating Him with contempt and mocking Him, dressed Him in a gorgeous robe and sent Him back to Pilate. **12** Now Herod and Pilate became friends with one another that very day; for before they had been enemies with each other. **13** Pilate summoned the chief priests and the rulers and the people, **14** and said to them, "You brought this man to me as one who incites the people to rebellion, and behold, having examined Him before you, I have found no guilt in this man regarding the charges which you make against Him. **15** "No, nor has Herod, for he sent Him back to us; and behold, nothing deserving death has been done by Him. **16** "Therefore I will punish Him and release Him." **17** [Now he was obliged to release to them at the feast one prisoner.] **18** But they cried out all together, saying, "Away with this man, and release for us Barabbas!" **19** (He was one who had been thrown into prison for an insurrection made in the city, and for murder.) **20** Pilate, wanting to release Jesus, addressed them again, **21** but they kept on calling out, saying, "Crucify, crucify Him!" **22** And he said to them the third time, "Why, what evil has this man done? I have found in Him no guilt demanding death; therefore I will punish Him and release Him." **23** But they were insistent, with loud voices asking that He be crucified. And their voices began to prevail. **24** And Pilate pronounced sentence that their demand be granted. **25** And he released the man they were asking for who had been thrown into prison for insurrection and murder, but he delivered Jesus to their will. **26** When they led Him away, they seized a man, Simon of Cyrene, coming in from the country, and placed on him the cross to carry behind Jesus.

• •

32 Two others also, who were criminals, were being led away to be put to death with Him. **33** When they came to the place called The Skull, there they crucified Him and the criminals, one on the right and the other on the left. **34** But Jesus was saying, "Father, forgive them; for they do not know what they are doing." And they cast lots, dividing up His garments among themselves. **35** And the people stood by, looking on. And even the rulers were sneering at Him, saying, "He saved others; let Him save Himself if this is the Christ of God, His Chosen One." **36** The soldiers also mocked Him, coming up to Him, offering Him sour wine, **37** and saying, "If You are the King of the Jews, save Yourself!" **38** Now there was also an inscription above Him, "THIS IS THE KING OF THE JEWS." **39** One of the criminals who were hanged there was hurling abuse at Him, saying, "Are You not the Christ? Save Yourself and us!" **40** But the other answered, and rebuking him said, "Do you not even fear God, since you are under the same sentence of condemnation? **41** "And we indeed are suffering justly, for we are receiving what we deserve for our deeds; but this man has done nothing wrong." **42** And he was saying, "Jesus, remember me when You come in Your kingdom!" **43** And He said to him, "Truly I say to you, today you shall be with Me in Paradise." **44** It was now about the sixth hour, and darkness fell over the whole land until the ninth hour, **45** because the sun was obscured; and the veil of the temple was torn in two. **46** And Jesus, crying out with a loud voice, said, "Father, into Your hands I commit My spirit." Having said this, He breathed His last. **47** Now when the centurion saw what had happened, he began praising God, saying, "Certainly this man was innocent." **48** And all the crowds who came together for this spectacle, when they observed what had happened, began to return, beating their breasts. **49** And all His acquaintances and the women who accompanied Him from Galilee were standing at a distance, seeing these things.

Jesus Is Innocent (23:1–16)

As chapter 23 opens, Luke notes Jesus' accusers. "Them" in verse 1 refers to the chief priests, scribes, and temple council mentioned in Luke 22:66. These Jewish leaders took Jesus to Pontius Pilate because he was the governor of Judea and had the authority to exercise capital punishment. With the land occupied by the Romans, the Jewish leaders themselves did not have the legal authority to execute Jesus based on religious charges of blasphemy. The Romans would allow execution if the charges presented a political accusation. Therefore, the Jewish leaders accused Jesus of subverting the nation and of opposing the payment of taxes. However, these charges had no basis, for Jesus was a teacher of peace and did not teach such things (see 20:20–26). Finally, the Jewish religious leaders brought against Jesus the political charge of calling himself a messianic king, an anointed king.

Luke did not record a reaction of Pilate to the politically oriented accusations. He did, however, record Pilate's question, "Are You the King of the Jews?" A play on words took place when Jesus answered the question. In verse 2, the religious leaders presented the charge that Jesus was calling himself "a King," meaning *an anointed king*, a religious title. In verse 3, Pilate ignored the religious part of the claim and asked Jesus whether he was "the King of the Jews." When Jesus provided no explanation, Pilate said that he could not find a charge against Jesus. Jesus was found innocent!

In verse 5, the religious leaders again attempted their initial charge against Jesus of causing political unrest. When they identified Jesus as having done this in Galilee, Pilate decided to send Jesus to Herod, who ruled Galilee (23:6–7).

Herod was familiar with the stories about Jesus and was eager to see for himself whether indeed Jesus was a miracle worker. However, Jesus refused to answer his questions.

So, in 23:1–16, the religious leaders and the soldiers of Herod ridiculed and mocked Jesus as a way to gain a sense of status and importance before the crowd. Herod and Pilate formed a friendship for the purpose of political gain. Jesus was found innocent by Herod as well. Pilate clearly stated that Jesus had done nothing to deserve death.

Jesus Replaces Barabbas (23:17–26)

With the people now on their side, the Jewish leaders called again for Jesus' execution and the release of Barabbas. For a third time Pilate declared Jesus' innocence, and for a third time they demanded the death penalty. At this point Pilate appeared less interested in justice than in crowd control. He moved to grant the crowd their wishes.

Barabbas was in prison for political insurrection and for murder (23:19, 25). According to the Roman legal system, Barabbas met the criteria for crucifixion. Instead, Jesus took his place.

Jesus Is Mocked (23:32–43).

Luke records that two other men, unknown to us, were led away for crucifixion as well. It was less work for the soldiers if several convicts were executed at once.[1] When they arrived at the place of crucifixion, the two men were crucified alongside Jesus, one on the left side and the other one on the right.

From the cross, Jesus uttered the words, "Father, forgive them, for they do not know what they are doing" (Luke 23:34). In doing so, Jesus practiced his own teaching of loving one's enemies (6:22–23, 27, 35).

The crucifixion was carried out by Roman soldiers. "Them" in Luke 24:34 likely referred to everyone involved in Jesus' death. This text alone dispels anti-Semitism as *all* were involved. The subsequent casting of lots over Jesus' clothes shows fulfillment of a messianic psalm (Ps. 22:18).

Jesus was mocked by people from three different groups in society. The religious rulers ridiculed Jesus for saving others and yet claiming he was the Christ. This represented religious mockery. The Roman soldiers ridiculed Jesus on a political level, aiming at the title "King of the Jews." This mockery was the accusation on the *titulus*, the charge written above the cross—"THIS IS THE KING OF THE JEWS" (Luke 23:38).

Also, one of the criminals hanging on a cross next to Jesus mocked him by saying, "Are You not the Christ? Save Yourself and us!" (23:39). The other criminal, like Pilate and Herod, declared Jesus' innocence. Having confessed his guilt, the criminal asked Jesus to "remember him" (23:41–42). Of everyone involved, this sorrowful criminal recognized who Jesus was—his Savior! Jesus responded by declaring, "Today you shall be with Me in Paradise" (23:43). The concept of "today" already was introduced by Luke in Luke 2:11 where the term "today" was used in the sense of "the beginning of the time of messianic salvation."[2] Likewise, when Jesus used the term "today" in Luke 4:21, he likely did not claim that the Scripture read from Isaiah (Luke 4:18–19) was fulfilled in that one day. Rather, the Scripture was fulfilled in the life and ministry of Christ. Thus the word "today" in Luke 23:43 seems to refer to the entire event of Jesus' atonement—his death and his upcoming resurrection.

In Jesus' time, the idea of *paradise* reminded the Jewish people of the Garden of Eden (Genesis 2:8; 13:10; Ezekiel 31:8) and of a future restoration in which the wilderness would become an Eden, the "garden" (Isaiah 51:3).[3] In the New Testament, *paradise* is used to refer to a final dwelling place of the righteous (2 Corinthians 12:4; Revelation 2:7). Here in Luke 23:43, the term seems to be used in the same New Testament sense—the criminal would be *saved.*

Jesus Dies (23:44–49)

The sixth hour was at noon, the brightest time of the day. The ninth hour was 3:00 pm. A first-century person would have interpreted the coming of darkness and the sun's waning as omens. Ancient Roman historians often reported such signs prior to the deaths of emperors or other significant people.

The curtain of the temple was traditionally understood to refer to the curtain at the entry of the holy of holies, the most inner part of the temple. With the curtain torn, all people could enter. Thus no longer was God's presence reserved for the Jewish high priest (Exodus 26:33). In the Old Testament law, the high priest alone could enter into the holy of holies where, according to the people's understanding, God dwelled. An alternate explanation is that the torn curtain, in the understanding of the people, meant God was no longer confined behind a curtain in a temple but now moved among his people. The temple system was now designated *out of order.*

Implications and Actions

As we journey through Luke's account of Jesus' crucifixion, we learn of Jesus' innocence, his endurance of cruel mockery, his compassion amidst pain, and his earth-shaking death. Each aspect of Jesus' crucifixion demonstrates that he died so that others might live.

Is the crucifixion important? In the gospel story itself, we learn of both Barabbas, the criminal on the cross, and the centurion. Their lives were spared or else changed forever. Furthermore, we learn that Jesus' crucifixion was the one and sufficient atonement for all people who would believe. As Jesus died, the veil to the most holy place was torn. The crucifixion opened the way for us to know God and for God to dwell among us intimately. Thus the crucifixion of Jesus Christ was the turning point in human history.

As we study and understand the crucifixion, we need to believe and accept Christ's atonement as fully sufficient for our salvation. Moreover, we must live daily in utter humility and gratitude for God's love shown in Christ. Finally, we must share this gospel with people so that they might understand the cross and experience God's salvation, rich and free.

JESUS' CRUCIFIXION

The manner of Jesus' death, crucifixion, was one of shame and disgrace. Even the actual place was an indication of shame. Luke 23:26, 32 mentions that Jesus and the two criminals were *led away* for crucifixion. John explains that the place where the crucifixion occurred was "near the city" (John 19:20).

On the Day of Atonement, the carcasses of the sacrificial animals were destroyed outside of the camp, outside the sacred area (Leviticus 16:27). Furthermore, those guilty of intentional sin were considered guilty of blasphemy, which was punishable by execution outside the camp (Lev. 24:11–

14; Numbers 15:30–36). Jesus was accused of blasphemy (Luke 22:70–71) and was executed outside Jerusalem (that is, outside the holy camp). Hebrews says: "For the bodies of those animals whose blood is brought into the holy place by the high priest as an offering for sin, are burned outside the camp. Therefore Jesus also, that He might sanctify the people through His own blood, suffered outside the gate. So, let us go out to Him outside the camp, bearing His reproach" (Heb. 13:11–13).

CONSIDER THIS

In Luke 23:

- Jesus was accused falsely three times

- Jesus was declared innocent three times

- So that "if anyone sins, we have an Advocate with the Father, Jesus Christ the righteous" (1 John 2:1)

QUESTIONS

1. What became the charge for Jesus' crucifixion? Was it a legitimate charge? Why or why not?

2. Had you been there in the crowd that day when Jesus was returned to Pilate, would you have cried out for the release of Barabbas or for the release of Jesus?

3. Although not plainly stated in the text, we can conjecture that the crowds that day were stirred up by the religious leaders. Peer pressure is nothing new. When do we encounter similar pressures in daily living that keep us from standing up for the core beliefs of our faith, such as the belief in the crucifixion of Jesus for our sins?

4. Imagine that you are Barabbas, sitting alone on the evening of the crucifixion. You reflect on Jesus' sacrifice. How does this affect your life?

NOTES —————————————————————————

1. Craig Keener, *IVP Background Commentary: New Testament* (Downers Grove: InterVarsity Press, 1994), 254.

2. Robert H. Stein, *Luke*, The New American Commentary, vol. 24 (Nashville, Tennessee: Broadman Press, 1992), 108.

3. John Nolland, *Luke 18:35–24:53*,Word Biblical Commentary, vol. 35c (Dallas, Texas: Word Publisher, 1993), 1152.

LESSON EIGHTEEN

Resurrected—for Us

MAIN IDEA

Jesus' resurrection shows he is truly the Christ of God, the fulfillment of God's promises in Scripture.

QUESTION TO EXPLORE

What makes Jesus' resurrection so important?

STUDY AIM

To state what Jesus' resurrection shows about who Jesus is, what Jesus does, and how I am to respond

QUICK READ

The Gospel of Luke mentions three groups of witnesses to the resurrection. Jesus commissioned the disciples to be witnesses to all nations.

The unthinkable happened at the funeral for Soviet Supreme leader Leonid Brezhnev in November 1982. Brezhnev was the latest in a line of rugged, atheistic Communist dictators. His funeral, one might suppose, would be the last place to witness an act of faith. But, just as the soldiers reached to close the lid of the coffin, Brezhnev's wife, overcome with emotion and perhaps faith, quickly reached down and made the sign of the cross on Brezhnev's chest.[1] Her act lingered as a sign of faith in God and a criticism against Communism and atheism's ultimate failure to provide meaning in life.

Today's world is full of people who choose not to believe in God and the hope found in Jesus Christ. Yet, in dark and hopeless moments, many of these same people find their hearts longing for meaning.

I (Ronnie Hood), for example, vividly remember sitting in the break room of a public school in Moscow, Russia, some years ago. I was serving as a missionary teacher of English in the public school system in Moscow. Surprisingly, the teachers raised the issue of belief in Christ during one of our many late afternoon tea times. I will never forget the command given me by the school principal, Natalia, in a moment of desperation, "Show me now why you believe that I might believe!"

The answers she longed to hear are found in the details of our Scripture passage today. The Scriptures were and are our witnesses, as were the women and the other disciples who encountered the risen Christ that first Sunday morning after the cross.

LUKE 24:1–10, 33–39, 44–48

1 But on the first day of the week, at early dawn, they came to the tomb bringing the spices which they had prepared. **2** And they found the stone rolled away from the tomb, **3** but when they entered, they did not find the body of the Lord Jesus. **4** While they were perplexed about this, behold, two men suddenly stood near them in dazzling clothing; **5** and as the women were terrified and bowed their faces to the ground, the men said to them, "Why do you seek the living One among the dead? **6** "He is not here, but He has risen. Remember how He spoke to you while He was still in Galilee, **7** saying that the Son of Man must be delivered into the hands of sinful men, and be crucified, and the third day rise again." **8** And they remembered His words, **9** and returned from the tomb and reported all these things to the eleven and to all the rest. **10** Now they were Mary Magdalene and Joanna and Mary the mother of James; also the other women with them were telling these things to the apostles.

• • • • • • • • • • • • • • • • • • • •

33 And they got up that very hour and returned to Jerusalem, and found gathered together the eleven and those who were with them, [34] saying, "The Lord has really risen and has appeared to Simon." [35] They began to relate their experiences on the road and how He was recognized by them in the breaking of the bread. [36] While they were telling these things, He Himself stood in their midst. [37] But they were startled and frightened and thought that they were seeing a spirit. [38] And He said to them, "Why are you troubled, and why do doubts arise in your hearts? [39] "See My hands and My feet, that it is I Myself; touch Me and see, for a spirit does not have flesh and bones as you see that I have."

•   •

[44] Now He said to them, "These are My words which I spoke to you while I was still with you, that all things which are written about Me in the Law of Moses and the Prophets and the Psalms must be fulfilled." [45] Then He opened their minds to understand the Scriptures, [46] and He said to them, "Thus it is written, that the Christ would suffer and rise again from the dead the third day, [47] and that repentance for forgiveness of sins would be proclaimed in His name to all the nations, beginning from Jerusalem. [48] "You are witnesses of these things. . . ."

The Women as Witnesses to the Resurrection (24:1–10)

On Easter morning, our eight-year-old daughter, Anastasia, was getting herself ready for the sunrise service at church. The night before, she and her six-year-old brother were excited about the prospect of getting up early to go to church while it was still dark, waiting for the sun to rise, and celebrating that Jesus rose from the dead. However, when reality struck the next morning and she realized how tired she was as she was getting dressed, the enthusiasm faded somewhat. Yet she put on her Easter dress and darted into the car. As we drove away toward the church in the early morning hours, Anastasia exclaimed, "Mommy, Jesus sure rose early, didn't he?"

Indeed, it was early in the morning when the women headed to the tomb. They had brought spices to embalm a dead body. Their Lord had died.

Further detail regarding these women is provided in verse 10. Women were the ones responsible for the burial procedures that involved rubbing the body with spices and perfume. Since this meant touching a dead body, it rendered people unclean. Thus women were the ones to perform this lowly task. Ironically, the women were the ones who first witnessed the resurrection. Recall Jesus' saying: "For the one who is least among all of you, this is the one who is great" (Luke 9:48b).

The grave was a cave-like tomb with a circular stone in front of the opening. The stone was rolled down a channel to close or open the grave.[2] The declaration about finding the body missing was earth-shattering. Was it stolen? The answer follows in the next verses.

As the women were "perplexed"—puzzled—about the absence of the body of Jesus, "two men" appeared to them (24:4). In verse 23, the men are referred to as "angels." They questioned the women as to why they sought the living in a tomb (see Luke 20:38). As the angels exhorted the women here, an angel also exhorted Mary in the birth story (1:26–38). As in the birth story, the exhortation pertained to life from God. The women recalled Jesus' words about his upcoming betrayal, suffering, death, and rising (9:22, 44; 18:31–33). The phrase, "He has risen," in Luke 24:6, may be more precisely translated as, *He has been raised [by God]*. This announcement explained why the tomb was empty. The announcement also declared the Easter message—Jesus is risen!

The three women were Mary Magdalene, Joanna, and Mary, the mother of James. Mary Magdalene and Joanna first were named in Luke 8:1–3. The grammar of the original language helps identify the third woman, Mary, as most likely the mother of James. This Mary is likewise identified as the mother of James in Mark 15:40; 16:1, confirming the relationship. Since the three women were mentioned by name, they likely were leading women. Additional women were present, joining these three women to relate the events of the resurrection to the apostles. The women's witness, however, was rejected (Luke 24:11).

The Disciples as Witnesses to the Resurrection (24:33–39)

Jesus revealed himself to two of the disciples who were headed to Emmaus from Jerusalem (24:31). At first they did not recognize him. When they related what had taken place in Jerusalem, Jesus shared with them the witness of the Old Testament (24:18–27). Jesus stayed with the disciples in Emmaus (hospitality was a main social feature in the culture). He took on the role of the head of the household when he broke bread during a meal gathering, at which point the disciples recognized him (24:35).

They (the two disciples to whom the resurrected Jesus appeared on the road to Emmaus) were now returning to Jerusalem. The eleven mentioned here are the same as those mentioned in verse 9. At this time, Judas had not been replaced. Once in Jerusalem, the three groups reunited—the two disciples, the eleven, and "the others," found in verse 9. The two disciples confessed their faith in the resurrected Christ and shared the encounter they had with Jesus. They exclaimed, "The Lord has risen indeed, and he has appeared to Simon!" (24:34, NRSV). In doing so, they confirmed what the women had proclaimed but what the disciples had failed to believe—Jesus indeed had risen from the dead! The Gospel of Luke emphasizes in verses 34–36 that while the disciples were still recalling their encounter with the resurrected Christ, he appeared in their midst. Confessing Christ leads to experiencing his very presence.

Like the women at the grave in Luke 24:5, the male disciples were frightened at the sight of Jesus. Jesus knew that the source of the disciples' doubt was disbelief in the mind. By calling attention to his hands and feet and inviting the disciples to touch and see, Jesus assured the disciples that his body was of flesh and blood (24:38). Thus, Jesus removed the fear that he was some sort of ghostly appearance (24:37) and discounted the claims that his appearance was merely spiritual in nature. Jesus made a strong statement here in the original Greek language, stating that it was he himself (that is, not an apparition or another version of him)!

The Scriptures as Witnesses to the Resurrection (24:44–48)

Verse 44 does not just speak concerning Jesus' showing his disciples that he truly was risen (the appearances to the women, Simon, the eleven, the disciples on the road to Emmaus, the confirmation of his physical resurrection, etc.). Rather the verse refers to the entire sequence of events of the passion—his suffering, his death, and his resurrection. In other words, by recalling his words before the passion, Jesus showed the disciples that he was the same Jesus who had foretold all these events. Jesus linked all that had occurred in his passion to Old Testament prophecies about the Messiah. Jesus interpreted the Scriptures through his life. This incident shows that Jesus was in control. He was the one providing access to understanding.

Next, after Jesus had opened the disciples' minds, he reminded them of what was written in the Scriptures, "that the Christ would suffer and rise again from the dead the third day, and that repentance for forgiveness of sins would be proclaimed in His name to all the nations, beginning from Jerusalem" (24:46–47).

Luke records Jesus' commission to proclaim forgiveness and repentance to all nations. This commission is specified in Acts 1:8, ". . . and you shall be My witnesses both in Jerusalem, and in all Judea and Samaria, and even to the remotest part of the earth." Luke viewed the role of disciples as witnesses of the resurrected Jesus. Specifically, they were witnesses of the things mentioned in Luke 24:46–47.

Implications and Actions

In chapter 24 of Luke's Gospel, we find various disciples struggling to comprehend Christ's resurrection from the dead. However, the risen Jesus carefully ministered to each in light of their particular needs, providing physical evidence and reminding them that the entire passion and resurrection was God's plan all along.

As we place ourselves in Luke's story of Jesus' passion and resurrection, our own doubts subside and our hearts are strengthened with belief that cannot be shaken. We see the women who witnessed the angels and the empty tomb. Then we journey with the Emmaus disciples who experienced Jesus' post-resurrection hospitality. Suddenly, we notice along with the other disciples the clear link between Jesus' passion and Old Testament prophecies. We gain confidence that the Jesus of the cross is the same Jesus who is alive today.

Today's world is full of hopeless people who need to hear the gospel of the living Lord. Therefore, witnesses must share their personal experiences with the resurrected Christ and teach the words of the gospel. May we testify today that Jesus' resurrection shows that Jesus is alive, Jesus is the answer to sin's ravages, and Jesus is the only way for humankind to come to the Father.

WITNESSES

A witness is a person who can testify to the truth in court. According to Old Testament law, several witnesses were needed to convict a person of any iniquity or sin (Deuteronomy 17:6–7; 19:15; Numbers 35:30). At times, inanimate objects were used as a witness as well (Joshua 24:27).

The Israelites were supposed to be witnesses by representing God's mission (Isaiah 43:10–12; 44:8). Jesus extended that same commission to his disciples (Luke 24:48). The disciples who would take the gospel into the world were also witnesses to the resurrection.

Ironically, the very first witnesses to the empty grave of Jesus were those whom society deemed least valuable—women. At that time Jewish people considered the testimony of women inadmissible in court.[3] Therefore, at first the Jewish male disciples did not believe the women (24:10–11). However, in the kingdom of God, society's rules and prejudices do not apply (9:48)! Thus the women and the male disciples, along with the Scriptures, were all valid witnesses to the resurrection.

CONSIDER THIS

Without Jesus' resurrection:
- We are without hope (Acts 24:15)
- We are false witnesses (1 Corinthians 15:15)
- We have a worthless faith (1 Cor. 15:17)
- We are still in our sins (1 Cor. 15:17)

With Jesus' resurrection:
- We are dead to sin and alive to God in Christ Jesus (Romans 6:11)
- We have victory through our Lord Jesus Christ (1 Cor. 15:57)
- We are born again to a living hope (1 Peter 1:3)
- We are blessed and holy (Revelation 20:6)

QUESTIONS

1. Would you have believed the women when they reported that Jesus had risen from the dead? Why or why not?

2. When you share the gospel, what role does the resurrection play in that presentation? Is the resurrection essential? Explain.

3. Is the Jesus of these Scriptures—the one who conquered death— the same Jesus with whom you walk your daily journey of faith? In what sense?

4. How should we view a Christian's death?

NOTES

1. Gary Thomas, "Wise Christians Clip Obituaries," *Christianity Today* (Oct. 3, 1994): 26. See also http://www.maxlucado.com/email/2006/07.07.html/

2. Robert H. Stein, *Luke*, The New American Commentary, vol. 24 (Nashville, Tennessee: Broadman Press, 1992), 604.

3. Josephus, *Antiquities of the Jews*, 4.8.15.

Our Next New Study

(Available for use beginning April 11, 2010)

THE BOOK OF GENESIS:
People Relating to God

Additional Resources for Studying *Genesis: People Relating to God*[1]

Walter Brueggemann. *Genesis*. Interpretation, A Bible Commentary for Teaching and Preaching. Atlanta: John Knox Press, 1982.

Terence Fretheim. "The Book of Genesis." *The New Interpreter's Bible*. Volume 1. Nashville: Abingdon Press, 1994.

Victor P. Hamilton. *The Book of Genesis: Chapters 1—17*. The New International Commentary on the Old Testament. Grand Rapids, Michigan: William B. Eerdmans Publishing Company, 1990.

Victor P. Hamilton. *The Book of Genesis: Chapters 18—50*. The New International Commentary on the Old Testament. Grand Rapids, Michigan: William B. Eerdmans Publishing Company, 1995.

Gerhard von Rad. *Genesis. A Commentary*. Revised Edition. Translated by John H. Marks. The Old Testament Library. Philadelphia: Westminster Press, 1972.

Gordon J. Wenham. *Genesis 1—15*. Word Biblical Commentary. Volume 1. Waco, Texas: Word Books, Publisher, 1987.

Gordon J. Wenham. *Genesis 16—50*. Word Biblical Commentary. Volume 2. Waco, Texas: Word Books, Publisher, 1994.

Additional Future Adult Bible Studies

Living Faith in Daily Life   For use beginning June 2010

Letters of James, Peter,   For use beginning
and John   September 2010

N O T E S ──────────────────────────────────

1   Listing a book does not imply full agreement by the writers or
    BAPTISTWAY PRESS® with all of its comments.

How to Order More Bible Study Materials

It's easy! Just fill in the following information. For additional Bible study materials available both in print and online, see www.baptistwaypress.org, or get a complete order form of available print materials—including Spanish materials—by calling 1-866-249-1799 or e-mailing baptistway@bgct.org.

Title of item	Price	Quantity	Cost
This Issue:			
The Gospel of Luke—Study Guide (BWP001085)	$4.45	_____	_____
The Gospel of Luke—Large Print Study Guide (BWP001086)	$4.85	_____	_____
The Gospel of Luke—Teaching Guide (BWP001087)	$4.85	_____	_____
Additional Issues Available:			
Growing Together in Christ—Study Guide (BWP001036)	$3.25	_____	_____
Growing Together in Christ—Large Print Study Guide (BWP001037)	$3.55	_____	_____
Growing Together in Christ—Teaching Guide (BWP001038)	$3.75	_____	_____
Participating in God's Mission—Study Guide (BWP001077)	$3.55	_____	_____
Participating in God's Mission—Large Print Study Guide (BWP001078)	$3.95	_____	_____
Participating in God's Mission—Teaching Guide (BWP001079)	$3.95	_____	_____
Genesis 12—50: Family Matters—Study Guide (BWP000034)	$1.95	_____	_____
Genesis 12—50: Family Matters—Teaching Guide (BWP000035)	$2.45	_____	_____
Leviticus, Numbers, Deuteronomy—Study Guide (BWP000053)	$2.35	_____	_____
Leviticus, Numbers, Deuteronomy—Large Print Study Guide (BWP000052)	$2.35	_____	_____
Leviticus, Numbers, Deuteronomy—Teaching Guide (BWP000054)	$2.95	_____	_____
Joshua, Judges—Study Guide (BWP000047)	$2.35	_____	_____
Joshua, Judges—Large Print Study Guide (BWP000046)	$2.35	_____	_____
Joshua, Judges—Teaching Guide (BWP000048)	$2.95	_____	_____
1 and 2 Samuel—Study Guide (BWP000002)	$2.35	_____	_____
1 and 2 Samuel—Large Print Study Guide (BWP000001)	$2.35	_____	_____
1 and 2 Samuel—Teaching Guide (BWP000003)	$2.95	_____	_____
1 and 2 Kings: Leaders and Followers—Study Guide (BWP001025)	$2.95	_____	_____
1 and 2 Kings: Leaders and Followers Large Print Study Guide (BWP001026)	$3.15	_____	_____
1 and 2 Kings: Leaders and Followers Teaching Guide (BWP001027)	$3.45	_____	_____
Ezra, Haggai, Zechariah, Nehemiah, Malachi—Study Guide (BWP001071)	$3.25	_____	_____
Ezra, Haggai, Zechariah, Nehemiah, Malachi—Large Print Study Guide (BWP001072)	$3.55	_____	_____
Ezra, Haggai, Zechariah, Nehemiah, Malachi—Teaching Guide (BWP001073)	$3.75	_____	_____
Job, Ecclesiastes, Habakkuk, Lamentations—Study Guide (BWP001016)	$2.75	_____	_____
Job, Ecclesiastes, Habakkuk, Lamentations—Large Print Study Guide (BWP001017)	$2.85	_____	_____
Job, Ecclesiastes, Habakkuk, Lamentations—Teaching Guide (BWP001018)	$3.25	_____	_____
Psalms and Proverbs—Study Guide (BWP001000)	$2.75	_____	_____
Psalms and Proverbs—Teaching Guide (BWP001002)	$3.25	_____	_____
Matthew: Hope in the Resurrected Christ—Study Guide (BWP001066)	$3.25	_____	_____
Matthew: Hope in the Resurrected Christ—Large Print Study Guide (BWP001067)	$3.55	_____	_____
Matthew: Hope in the Resurrected Christ—Teaching Guide (BWP001068)	$3.75	_____	_____
Mark: Jesus' Works and Words—Study Guide (BWP001022)	$2.95	_____	_____
Mark: Jesus' Works and Words—Large Print Study Guide (BWP001023)	$3.15	_____	_____
Mark:Jesus' Works and Words—Teaching Guide (BWP001024)	$3.45	_____	_____
Jesus in the Gospel of Mark—Study Guide (BWP000066)	$1.95	_____	_____
Jesus in the Gospel of Mark—Large Print Study Guide (BWP000065)	$1.95	_____	_____
Jesus in the Gospel of Mark—Teaching Guide (BWP000067)	$2.45	_____	_____
Luke: Journeying to the Cross—Study Guide (BWP000057)	$2.35	_____	_____
Luke: Journeying to the Cross—Large Print Study Guide (BWP000056)	$2.35	_____	_____
Luke: Journeying to the Cross—Teaching Guide (BWP000058)	$2.95	_____	_____
The Gospel of John: The Word Became Flesh—Study Guide (BWP001008)	$2.75	_____	_____
The Gospel of John: The Word Became Flesh—Large Print Study Guide (BWP001009)	$2.85	_____	_____
The Gospel of John: The Word Became Flesh—Teaching Guide (BWP001010)	$3.25	_____	_____
Acts: Toward Being a Missional Church—Study Guide (BWP001013)	$2.75	_____	_____
Acts: Toward Being a Missional Church—Large Print Study Guide (BWP001014)	$2.85	_____	_____
Acts: Toward Being a Missional Church—Teaching Guide (BWP001015)	$3.25	_____	_____
Romans: What God Is Up To—Study Guide (BWP001019)	$2.95	_____	_____
Romans: What God Is Up To—Large Print Study Guide (BWP001020)	$3.15	_____	_____
Romans: What God Is Up To—Teaching Guide (BWP001021)	$3.45	_____	_____
Galatians and 1&2 Thessalonians—Study Guide (BWP001080)	$3.55	_____	_____
Galatians and 1&2 Thessalonians—Large Print Study Guide (BWP001081)	$3.95	_____	_____
Galatians and 1&2 Thessalonians—Teaching Guide (BWP001082)	$3.95	_____	_____

Ephesians, Philippians, Colossians—Study Guide (BWP001060)	$3.25	_____	_____
Ephesians, Philippians, Colossians—Large Print Study Guide (BWP001061)	$3.55	_____	_____
Ephesians, Philippians, Colossians—Teaching Guide (BWP001062)	$3.75	_____	_____
1, 2 Timothy, Titus, Philemon—Study Guide (BWP000092)	$2.75	_____	_____
1, 2 Timothy, Titus, Philemon—Large Print Study Guide (BWP000091)	$2.85	_____	_____
1, 2 Timothy, Titus, Philemon—Teaching Guide (BWP000093)	$3.25	_____	_____
Revelation—Study Guide (BWP000084)	$2.35	_____	_____
Revelation—Large Print Study Guide (BWP000083)	$2.35	_____	_____
Revelation—Teaching Guide (BWP000085)	$2.95	_____	_____

Coming for use beginning April 11, 2010

(Genesis: People Relating to God is an 8-session study)

Genesis: People Relating to God—Study Guide (BWP001088)	$2.35	_____	_____
Genesis: People Relating to God—Large Print Study Guide (BWP001089)	$2.75	_____	_____
Genesis: People Relating to God—Teaching Guide (BWP001090)	$2.95	_____	_____

Standard (UPS/Mail) Shipping Charges*			
Order Value	Shipping charge**	Order Value	Shipping charge**
$.01—$9.99	$6.50	$160.00—$199.99	$22.00
$10.00—$19.99	$8.00	$200.00—$249.99	$26.00
$20.00—$39.99	$9.00	$250.00—$299.99	$28.00
$40.00—$59.99	$10.00	$300.00—$349.99	$32.00
$60.00—$79.99	$11.00	$350.00—$399.99	$40.00
$80.00—$99.99	$12.00	$400.00—$499.99	$48.00
$100.00—$129.99	$14.00	$500.00—$599.99	$58.00
$130.00—$159.99	$18.00	$600.00—$799.99	$70.00**

Cost
of items (Order value) _____

Shipping charges
(see chart*) _____

TOTAL _____

*Plus, applicable taxes for individuals and other taxable entities (not churches) within Texas will be added. Please call 1-866-249-1799 if the exact amount is needed prior to ordering.

**For order values $800.00 and above, please call 1-866-249-1799 or check www.baptistwaypress.org

Please allow three weeks for standard delivery. For express shipping service: Call 1-866-249-1799 for information on additional charges.

YOUR NAME _____   PHONE _____

YOUR CHURCH _____   DATE ORDERED _____

SHIPPING ADDRESS _____

CITY _____   STATE _____   ZIP CODE _____

E-MAIL _____

MAIL this form with your check for the total amount to
BAPTISTWAY PRESS, Baptist General Convention of Texas,
333 North Washington, Dallas, TX 75246-1798
(Make checks to "Baptist Executive Board.")

OR, **FAX** your order anytime to: 214-828-5376, and we will bill you.

OR, **CALL** your order toll-free: 1-866-249-1799
(M-Th 8:30 a.m.-6:00 p.m.; Fri 8:30 a.m.-5:00 p.m. central time),
and we will bill you.

OR, **E-MAIL** your order to our internet e-mail address:
baptistway@bgct.org, and we will bill you.

OR, **ORDER ONLINE** at www.baptistwaypress.org.

We look forward to receiving your order! Thank you!